# Upgrading Democracy

Claiming a Say to Achieve True Democracy

PETER MONIEN

Do we really want to continue
handing out blank cheques
to politicians for four years?

# DEDICATION

For all...

...who are disappointed by politics.

...who still want to change something.

...who have not given up yet.

...who are in search for a solution, a Plan B.

...who still hope.


Especially for...

...all non-voters who deliberately do not vote as they don't want to

legitimize a rigged system.

# CONTENTS

# Preface to the English Version of the book

Winston Churchill once said, "…democracy is the worst form of government except all those other forms that have been tried from time to time."

Most take this as an assurance that democracy is the best solution to govern a country.  But only few see it for what it is: A bad grade for the best solution we have so far and a call to improve its institutions.
This is badly needed.

Democracy as we have it today, is sure not what we hoped it would be.

Most countries have free elections. But, almost all of us would choose not to be represented by the elected parties. Studies show that this impression is right. Political decisions very often reflect the will of the upper class and at best, ignore the middle and lower classes.

There are only a few countries that give voters the right to correct the decisions of the government and come up with proposals on their own. Normally, voters don't have any influence outside of elections. Of course, we have the option to spend years of our free time organizing and forcing the government to listen to us. But we have no right that this action will result in meaningful change.

Trust in politicians and in our democratic institution has been eroding for decades. Many of us have ceased to vote at all, because either: "It doesn't make a difference" or "There is no real alternative".

But what if there was an alternative that enabled citizens to have their voices heard and directly reflected in votes in parliament?

This book describes a practical suggestion to cure the weaknesses of a pure representative democracy. It shows a way to add direct democratic elements, even if the incumbent political parties stand in opposition.

The ideas outlined in this book are applicable to literally every political system worldwide. For the political systems provided, I focus on the United States of America along with the German system as well. This has gone a different route in many regards and is a more suitable example for many other countries.

# Introduction

The citizen feels powerless. Globalization is perceived as a force of nature that is inexorably changing his life. Emerging new technologies endanger his workplace. He feels disconnected and is afraid of social decline. According to an OECD publication[1] middle-class wages are rising much slower than the cost of living. 11% of middle-class households in OECD countries are over-indebted. A low, or even mid-level education is less likely to be sufficient enough to be in the middle class. Emerging new technologies endanger the workplace. The citizen feels detached and is afraid of social decline.

There is no addressee for this feeling of powerlessness[2]. Politicians of the big parties point out: "You can't stop market forces" and "One might as well try to stop the world turning." They refuse the citizen's right to decide for themselves on today's complex issues and merely decide for them.

---

[1] http://www.oecd.org/publications/under-pressure-the-squeezed-middle-class-689afed1-en.htm

[2] https://youtu.be/krNrjSFstQQ, Pia Mancini, Democracy Earth Foundation, Millennials and Democracy: Apathy and Noise

The voter is in demand every couple of years. He is asked to leave his vote in the ballot box. By doing so, he buries almost all the possibilities of influence that the political system grants him.

After the election, almost nothing changes for him. The voter often has the feeling of only being able to choose "The lesser evil." None of the established parties are developing a bold, long-term vision of a future worth being lived. The feeling of powerlessness causes many citizens to forgo voting altogether. Due to low trust, many voters turn to parties that provide simple answers, such as nationalist parties and their ideals of "The People" or "The Nation." In worst cases, anger erupts into violence and dominant groups turn against the weaker groups of their populations.

Meanwhile, the politicians interpret silence of the majority as consent. They deliberately ignore the ever-louder sound of teeth grinding.

As a result, the most important asset of our system and our country is lost: trust in institutions and democracy itself.

But it is still us who decide on our rules and systems. We can determine how we can use the strengths of capitalism. But we can also decide where to keep capitalism in check and decide where it is being misguided. For example, in the areas of social policy and the environment. It is up to us to find a better system and try it out together. A system, that does not place shareholder value and gross national product before the well-being of it's citizens.

Who says that we have to hand a blank check to politicians for four years? It is time for a new political system in which the citizen, the sovereign, has more say and has the corresponding powers. It is about intelligently sharing political power and introducing direct democratic elements. Democracy should not be an exception that occurs every four or five years. Important decisions should be made by the voters themselves, whereby they have to be enabled by neutral information.

But how can this democratization of politics be achieved if the political parties in power reject national referendums?

Why should the established parties partly give up their power?
What is a viable and achievable way in the current political party system to achieve this democratic change?

A Proxy Party would allow voters far more than to organize themselves to put pressure on politics. A Proxy Party would allow its members to directly take part in decisions. The much-needed positive change could be accelerated. Moreover, A Proxy Party's involvement in citizen's initiatives or other associations will bear more fruit and quicker through a parliamentary democratic champion.

I invite the reader to take a look at the shortcomings of the current political system and explain the need for democratic change. I outline a path that can be implemented in the current political system. This can lead us into a better democratic future. I offer concrete proposals for implementation. These should not be understood as dogmas, but rather as a basis for discussion.

The Democracy Index[3] doesn't list most of our democratic states as "full" but only as "flawed democracies". And this situation doesn't seem to improve. On the contrary almost all countries seem to cut back democratic rights faster than they improve upon them.

> "In 2017, the Turkish population voted to give greater power to their President Recep Tayyip Erdogan and increase his control over the judicial arm of government. In the same year, the Polish parliament

---

[3] https://en.wikipedia.org/wiki/Democracy_Index

passed legislation which removed the Supreme Court and allowed the legislature to appoint a new judiciary directly."[4]

This should remind us, that democracy itself is not a given. It is constantly under threat to be undermined and hollowed out. And new technologies make governing without the consent of the population increasingly more "manageable".

It's about time for politics to step into the 21st century. We should get our democratic act together and develop our political systems to boost democracy and become true "full democracies".

---

[4] Tony Bracks, Solving For Democracy: A democracy without politics, removing the problems that limit our government, p. 33

# Part I

# PROBLEMS

# 1. Crisis of representation

Confidence in the political system and politicians have been eroding for many years. The citizens go to the poll. After the election the following will happen:

1. In a multiparty election system, parties enter into a coalition, potentially one no voter really wanted.

2. In a multiparty election system, coalition negotiation leads to the write off of many election promises. These can only be partially enforced and not even make it into the coalition paper. If you live in the US or the UK or in another country with only two major parties, start from 3.

3. Decisions often seem less based on logic and common sense than on electoral promises, favors,…etc.

4. Lobbyists influence politicians.

5. Some important topics are handled in backroom deals.

6. Some important topics are not handled at all.

7. If something goes wrong, no person is responsible (organized irresponsibility).

8.  Representatives, their parliamentary staff, their political parties, the political groups,…etc. get a nice raise.

9.  Former politicians are hired in well-paid jobs as a reward.

This happens over and over again. In virtually every country. Worldwide.

Almost never does the "voice of the people" correct political decision. If at all, this happens through initiatives and NGOs. To achieve this, enough public pressure must be built for each topic. This is very time consuming. If they win, politicians answer by delaying the subject. And if the pressure is too high, give in to some small concessions. If the pressure gets higher than that, they implement changes that doesn't lead to real changes. On the flip side, they push their own agendas under another name or sneak it in another bill. Politically interested citizens are frustrated by these exhaustive tactics. They feel powerless and resign from politics altogether.

Only in a few countries, such as Switzerland, is the "electorate" asked on a national level on individual topics. In many countries nationwide, referendum doesn't even exist.

It is no wonder that politicians rank very low on the popularity scale. In the US, only 18% of Americans believe their government "almost always" (3%) or "most of the time" (15%) can be trusted.[5] It's no wonder that the population's disenchantment with politics is increasing every year. The *Edelman Trust Barometer*[6] states, "56% don't know which politician to trust." According to RepresentUS, only 4% of Americans have a "…great deal of confidence in congress." American voters are left with the choice between pest and cholera.

---

[5] http://www.people-press.org/2017/12/14/public-trust-in-government-1958-2017/
[6] https://www.edelman.com/sites/g/files/aatuss191/files/2018-10/2018_Edelman_Trust_Barometer_Global_Report_FEB.pdf

Many voters feel powerless. They vote every four years, but afterwards they can only stare wide-eyed at what the politicians make of it. The voter does not feel heard or represented and is, for the most part, right.

The views of the poor and middle class are irrelevant to US policy at best. A US study in 2012, *Affluence and Influence*[7], from Princeton University, came to similar conclusions:

> "With sharp analysis and an impressive range of data, Martin Gilens looks at thousands of proposed policy changes, and the degree of support for each among poor, middle-class, and affluent Americans. His findings are staggering: when preferences of low- or middle-income Americans diverge from those of the affluent, there is virtually no relationship between policy outcomes and the desires of less advantaged groups. In contrast, affluent Americans' preferences exhibit a substantial relationship with policy outcomes whether their preferences are shared by lower-income groups or not."

The Washington Post writes[8] in May 2016 during the presidential election campaign:

> "Many Americans voting for outsider candidates believe that government pretty much ignores people like them. We think they're right."

According to the Economists Intelligence's Unit Democracy Index[9], the United States is listed as a "flawed democracy."

---

[7] https://press.princeton.edu/titles/9836.html
[8] https://www.washingtonpost.com/news/monkey-cage/wp/2016/05/23/critics-challenge-our-portrait-of-americas-political-inequality-heres-5-ways-they-are-wrong/?noredirect=on
[9] https://www.economist.com/graphic-detail/2019/01/08/the-retreat-of-global-democracy-stopped-in-2018

A similar empirical study was conducted in Germany. It examined the approval rating of German citizens about 250 issues and their political implementation. It basically had the same findings as the US study. Only a fraction of the original 60-pages made it into the government report. Most of the findings were censored. The original document repeatedly mentioned a "crisis of representation" and also the influence of lobbyists.

The government report didn't mention these topics at all.


## Summary and questions

These surveys and studies prove the failure of the representation of the citizen by his elected representatives.

- How can such a distortion occur?
- What causes this non-representation of large classes of the population?
- What can be done politically to improve the current situation?
- Is there a shortcut to a more direct democratic system? How could this enable citizens to have a real say in political decisions?

## 2. Representational weakness of the political system

In almost all countries, voters can freely choose parties to represent. If the country has a majority election system (e.g. USA, Great Britain), the party with the most votes rules. When elected by proportional representation (e.g. Germany), the winning party almost always has to team up with another party. They have to form a coalition to have a stable majority in parliament.

It is assumed that the parties elected by the voter best assert the interests of their constituents.

However, as stated in the introduction, in reality, this is not the case for a vast majority of voters.

How does this happen?

a) A party can practically never represent the individual citizen 100%

In some countries you can use a web-based program to match your political believes with the election program of the political parties. After reviewing the 30 to 50 topics, you will hardly find a 100% match with any party. But this is not astounding. Voters are individuals and have individual opinions.

b) Only a few topics were previously coordinated with the citizen

Including ALL political issues in an election program is impossible. Even if it was possible, no voter would read multi-volume works, much less those of *several* parties. In this respect, the statements made by parties in the election program are limited to only a few main subject areas. For the rest, the voter has to trust his preferred party.

The voter does not only choose the election program, but also the underlying philosophy of the party. Many voters are drawn to the idealized identity of a party and not its truth. It's about belonging to a tribe with certain attitudes. Voting for his party partly defines the identity of the voter. Here it has to be kept in mind, that the reputation of the party does not necessarily correspond to reality. Even the name of the party can be deceiving. For most topics, the party will not be able to coordinate with its constituents. The elected representatives of the party will decide on most questions without really knowing the will of the electorate. In reality, the parties only work with assumptions; and these may well be far from reality.

c) Governing in a government coalition dilutes party goals

In a multiparty election system, it is almost always the case that the winning party cannot govern alone after the election. It has to bring a coalition partner on board. Only with this partner does the party have a governing majority in parliament. In this respect, neither of the two (or three) parties can implement all their self-defined goals. The parties are already aware of this before and may exaggerate their promises on purpose. They can then blame the other party for not being able to implement all their goals.

d) Representatives heavily depend on their party

Ruling a country is not easy. Many decisions have to be taken and legislative changes have to be decided. This diversity of topics cannot be covered by a single member. In this respect, every member of parliament depends on his party. The party must prepare the topic so that the members of parliament can educate themselves in a very short time to enable their decisions on a good factual basis.

Instead, all members of parliament are said to receive (a) too many, (b) too extensive, (c) too unstructured documentation that they (d) have to read in far too little time. Most of the representatives capitulate, only inform themselves superficially and finally follow the vote recommendation of their party.

Or the party chooses the shortcut and lets the representatives vote in blind trust that their party is doing it right. You can doubt if this does justice to the responsibility as a representative of his constituents.

It is frightening how few members know about essential facts and interrelations and how far away their "knowledge" is from reality. Surveys on the knowledge of the current monetary system show massive knowledge gaps in virtually all countries. This makes representatives easily "steerable."


e) As a party you add external expertise

With the number and breadth of topics just listed, no party alone can manage to deliver a good preparation for the topics to be voted on. To manage this in the very short time frame given to prepare drafts, the people who compile the basic papers are forced to draw on external advice. This is understandable and serves a purpose. After all, a decision should be made on the basis of valid facts and expertise.

Many organizations rightly criticize that the representatives are much more likely to meet with lobbyists than the representatives of citizen's initiatives or NGOs. It is also criticized that there is almost always a lack of transparency with whom the representatives meet to educate themselves about the topic. In this context, benefits handed to representatives during their time in parliament or after, are problematic, as these can influence decisions. This will be analyzed in Chapter 6 as one of the weak points of parliamentary democracy.

## f) Panels and committees

But where do the preparatory documents and information come from that the representatives receive? These are commissioned by the party leadership (to their liking) or are prepared in panels and committees. In Europe, an overwhelming majority of the laws come from Brussels. These are waved through in parliament. Otherwise, they would stop the parliamentary operation due to their massive quantity.

This power concentration is a perfect target for influence by influencer groups. It is one of the major weaknesses of parliamentary democracy. This will be detailed in Chapter 6.

## g) Faction coercion (whip)

The coalition must rely on the support of the representatives of its parties. Otherwise, it is not functional. If it doesn't succeed in this, it may not be able to get through their proposals in parliament nor pass the proposed legislation.

All constitutions state that the representative represents all people and is not bound by orders and instructions. He is only subject to his conscience. But de facto, there is a submission of the representatives to their party. The sociolo-gist Erwin K. Scherch, speaks of a "feudal system" characterized by the principle: "Exchange of privileges against loyalty".[10]

This coercion is called "whip" in British English. And for good reason. Deviators must reckon with a loss of their list position at the next election. In severe cases, they can also be excluded from their political group. Very few representatives dare to (even partially) not keep the faction discipline. This often results in a selection of the best adapted, rather than best candidates, for politics.

The whip may lead to the adoption of a law that has a low acceptance rate (even far less than 50% of the representatives). This is likely when the leadership threatens their own party with resignation or even an official: "vote of confidence."


h) Votes on important changes with few members

The rules of the legislative body (of most countries) will demand half of its members to be present in the meeting to have a quorum. This is for good reason. Decisions taken in small groups do not have a proven, clear democratic legitimacy. Constitutional lawyers rightly criticize legislation and practice[11] that allows easy exceptions from these rules. They would like to see at least half of the members sitting in plenary when laws are passed.

Silly to see a connection of the number of participants in voting on the popularity of legislative changes among the voters. After all, every member of parliament can later tell his constituents with fullest conviction that he was not present at this vote.

---

[10] Erwin K. Scherch, Cliquen, Klüngel und Karrieren, p. 117
[11] German: https://www.mdr.de/nachrichten/politik/inland/bundestag-gesetze-ohne-mehrheit-100.html

## Summary

It is very unlikely that a party represents the will of even one citizen 1: 1. The actual decisions are pre-decided using external expertise and small groups for preparation. These experts and preparatory groups are an optimal target to be influenced by external stakeholders. The representatives have minimal chances to disobey with the "guidance" of their party. The actual voting procedure with a small parliamentary group is an undemocratic, but often legal practice.

# 3. Power and distance from the citizen

Politics likes to refer to the foreseeable historical failure of the socialist and communist systems. The economic argument is something like this:

It is not surprising that these centrally planned systems did not work. Each centrally-created 5-year plan is doomed to fail right from the start. These plans are too far removed from the reality of business and citizens. Central data processing is far inferior to decentralize. Central processing lacks much information. Only the market can coordinate market participants efficiently. Therefore, a market driven economy (capitalism), is superior to a state-directed economy.

Confidence in the market as an efficient coordination mechanism and in the principle of subsidiarity is high. This principle states that anything a political level can accomplish on its own shouldn't be taken over by a higher-level organization. The municipalities decide on local issues. The federal states decide on state issues. The federal government decides on federal issues. And then, there is the EU. This is so detached from its citizens, that a majority of Europeans are for Europe, but not in favor of the EU [12]. EU-critical parties

---

[12] https://www.theguardian.com/world/2013/apr/24/trust-eu-falls-record-low

enjoy a massive popularity.

That might stem from the understanding of democracy of some EU officials. This is prominently reflected in the infamous quote by Jean-Claude Juncker, the President of the EU:

> "We decide on something, leave it lying around and wait and see what happens. If no one kicks up a fuss, because most people don't under-stand what has been decided, we continue step by step until there is no turning back."[13]

Recent developments, such as the wish to abandon unanimity, point to an increasing deterioration of the situation. The Anti-Spiegel analyzes the importance of the transfer of budget law to the EU level. This would mean

> "…that he wants to take this most important field of politics, on which everything else depends, out of democratic control and into the hands of bureaucrats and officials, whom no one democratically controls…Those who then decide about our money would sit in Brussels and are elected by no one."[14]

If you transfer the image of failure of central systems to politics, you get about the following presumable order:

Municipality Level → relatively close to the citizen; the policy is largely directed towards the citizen

→ Citizen satisfaction: very high to sufficient

---

[13] https://www.telegraph.co.uk/news/worldnews/europe/eu/10967168/Jean-Claude-Junckers-most-outrageous-political-quotations.html

[14] Translated from: https://www.anti-spiegel.ru/2019/kein-scherz-schaeuble-fordert-abschaffung-der-demokratie-und-niemand-protestiert/

State Level ➔ far away from the citizen; politics directed towards the citizen to a greater extent

➔ Citizen satisfaction: medium to sufficient

Federal Level ➔ very far away from the citizen; the policy is largely not directed towards the citizen

➔ Citizen satisfaction: medium to insufficient

EU Level ➔ furthest away from the citizen; the policy is only slightly directed towards the citizen

➔ Citizen satisfaction: poor to insufficient

The further the political level is removed from the citizen, the lower the agreement with the electoral will and the higher the dissatisfaction of the citizen.

This may only be judged as regrettable unless another factor is considered:

The higher the political level, the greater the influence their decisions have on citizens.

Here are just a few topics that are decided at the level of the EU or the federal government. All have an influence on the states and municipalities and heavily influence the lives of all citizens:

- Unemployment sanctions
- Surveillance laws
- Bank bailouts
- EU enlargement
- Energy transition / climate change
- Asylum and migration policy (+ UN added as one level above)
- Starting or joining a war

## Summary

Proximity to the citizen and his will decreases with the distance of the political institutions. The reverse is true of the influence of institutions at different levels. Decisions that have far-reaching consequences for the life of the citizen are taken by the Federal Government: far from the citizen (and very often also from his will). In the European case this doesn't get better with decisions taken on the EU level.

# 4. Power and lack of control

"With great power comes great responsibility."

-Richard Nixon

Politicians are given the power of legislature by their constituents. The government is entrusted with the power of the executive. Both have great responsibility. Both should be monitored and, if necessary, corrected by an effective system of control bodies and counterweights. This is the only way a healthy democracy can be guaranteed.

As the author Richard C. Lyons said in his book "The DNA of Democracy" and in a podcast interview: [15]

> "I think of democracy as the recessive gene and tyranny as the dominant gene. … Government by its nature concentrates power. Once you have power you can concentrate it. Once concentrated you have the means of defending it. Once you defend you have the means of expanding it. In democracy each individual has the responsibility to

---

[15] http://keepingdemocracyalive.com/the-dna-of-democracy-its-a-recessive-gene/

defend democracy."

According to this logic we need to be constantly alert and defend democracy. Said differently:

> "Freedom wears off if you don't use it."
> -Reinhard Mey, German singer

## 4.1 Voting with integrated funeral

The voter is asked to vote every four years. He goes to the polls and leaves his vote in the ballot box. Incidentally, the German wording is very precise. The citizen gives his vote to the political system and buries it (mostly with his hopes that it will get better this time) in the "Wahlurne" (direct translation: "voting-urn"). After that, he no longer has power over how the political apparatus acts on behalf of voters and how it spends their money.

## 4.2 Regulatory bodies and missing separation of powers

The political system often talks about control bodies and counterweights. They should balance the political system if it does not work as it should.

The separation of powers is intended to "limit the power of the individual organs, so that not all power is bundled in one state organ, e.g. the government. Power should be in the hands of different, mutually equal, organs. The most important safeguard against an increasing concentration of the various powers in one hand is the following: to provide the office holders of the various bodies with all the necessary constitutional means to ward off the infringement of others." [16]

The separation of powers is a cornerstone of democratic constitutional state

---

[16] Translated from: http://www.gewaltenteilung.de

construction. It should ensure that even incompetent state officials can cause as little damage as possible. Most important, it is installed to minimize the chance that something like Nazi Germany happens again. No political party should be able to take over the whole state and its institutions. Checks and balances are essential.

For a strong democracy, it is imperative that all three classical pillars of democracy are strong and independent from each other:

- Legislative (writing the laws)
- Judiciary (interpreting the laws and judging)
- Executive (enforcing the laws)

Germany is categorized as "full democracy" in the *Economist Intelligence Unit's Democracy Index*[17]. So, you might be astounded to hear that Germany has only two pillars instead of three. As explained by Udo Hochschild[18] the entire judiciary is under control of the government. They are "object to their decisions and committed to government loyalty." The German system relies on the principle of trust, in terms of case law, instead of a clean separation of powers. "It relies on the lawfulness and judgment of the party-political elite, who oversee and administer the judiciary and the subordinate officials." The request of the European Council[19] to introduce a system of self-administration of justice is ignored by the German politicians. Equally ignored is the demand for "abolishing the option that Justice Ministers give the prosecution instructions on individual cases." As Udo Hochschild closes, "The democratic constitutional state in Germany has an open flank."

But even if all three pillars are constructed correctly, institutions of most

---

[17] https://www.economist.com/graphic-detail/2019/01/08/the-retreat-of-global-democracy-stopped-in-2018
[18] Translated from: http://www.gewaltenteilung.de
[19] Translated from: http://www.gewaltenteilung.de/europarat-pressemitteilung/

countries still have a flaw built in:

**Head of a Chamber**, like the speaker of the US House of Representatives or the President of the German Bundestag

Never underestimate the power of someone that heads an assembly and guards its procedures. He is the one who decides if the assembly has a quorum. He might be able to decide on the order of the list of speakers. He can be friendly to your last-minute proposal or reject to include it in the meeting. Optimally he should treat all parties neutral and should be very strict with procedures.

Weakness: The Speaker/President is declared or at least traditionally prepositioned by the largest political party/faction. It can therefore be assumed that this person, at least in comparison to someone neutral, might be inclined to opt for the interests of his party. The established parties will tend to agree on a candidate who will not unduly question the parties' actions.

**Supreme Court** - The court monitors the compliance with the constitution. It assesses the constitutionality of the laws passed by the parliament (judicial review). It also checks whether decisions taken by the courts are in accordance with the constitution. Optimally, a judge is a true light bearer for democracy and will defend every attack that tries to dilute its institutions or rules.

System weakness: In the US, judges are nominated by the President. In Germany, they are nominated fifty-fifty by the house representing the federal and the one representing the state. It can be presumed that the appointed persons, at least in comparison to a neutral person, might be inclined to vote for the interests of their specific party. In a multiparty system the incumbent parties will tend to agree on a candidate who will not unduly question new laws, or the interpretation adopted by the parties.

**Government Accountability Office** - The US Government Accountability Office (GAO) and the German "Bundesrechnungshof," both examine the budget and economic management of the federal government[20]. Both write audit notes with concrete suggestions for quality improvements saving potential and/or additional revenue. Among other duties, they report to parliament on their most important audit results.

System weakness: The US Congress establishes a commission to recommend individuals to the President for the position of the Comptroller General of the GAO. The President appoints the Comptroller General. In Germany, the President and Vice President of the Bundesrechnungshof are elected fifty-fifty by the house representing the federal and the one representing the state level. The established parties will tend to agree on candidates who will not question the power of the parties too much.

The underlying theme becomes obvious: The controlled have power via the appointment of the positions of the institutions that control them. This, is an influence where there should not be.


**Press / Media** - According to the unofficial definition, press/media is "the fourth political power." This can also be described as a kind of "early warning system and security net of democracy." If the controls and security systems of the political system itself are inadequate, the media can expose the deficits and alert the public. The media should critically scrutinize the policies of parliament and the government to uncover issues that policymakers would

---

[20] https://www.gao.gov/about and translated from
https://www.bundesrechnungshof.de/de/bundesrechnungshof/organisation/aufg
aben

like to keep secret, especially when they act questionably or try to circumvent democratic processes altogether. The media should show backgrounds and embed the latest news in them. Facts and opinions are clearly to be separated. Media should enable citizens to form their own picture and make informed decisions.

System weakness: Many political parties own or control media or are associated with wealthy individuals who support their case. As described in Chapter 7.5, they thus have effective tools at their disposal to strongly influence public opinion.

**The Citizens** - The citizen is the sovereign. The party acts in his name. He chooses the party and can withdraw his trust every four years and elect a different party. If he does not like current decisions of the government, he can form or work on: initiatives, non-governmental organizations, associations,...etc. to protest. He can go out on the street and express his resentment loudly (Right of Demonstration).

System weakness: The citizen is not consulted outside of the election and is given no possibility of opposition. At least not on the most relevant level, the federal level. If he is willing to sacrifice much of his free time, he can engage in political activities. Together with others, he can sometimes successfully influence politics. However, it is easy for politicians to react with words rather than deeds and make only minor changes if the political pressure is not sustained for a long enough time.

## 4.3 The executive extending its rights and powers

Since 9/11, the security laws have been massively tightened. For critics, it seems that since 2001, only the mention of the phrase "war on terrorism," is sufficient to automatically suspend all fundamental rights.

The following three areas are considered particularly dangerous:

a)  Undetermined legal terms

These allow the police to interfere with fundamental rights, on a very vague basis. Terms such as "endangerment," "concrete danger," or "urgent danger," give the police too much freedom. In times of crisis, these can quickly lead to disproportionate restrictions on fundamental rights.

b)  Lack of privacy protection

Few effective measures and controls exist that ensure that the monitoring by the Federal Office Criminal Investigation and other organizations is appropriate and that only case relevant data is to be used. This is particularly important as the modern telecommunications monitoring, offers far-reaching possibilities especially the direct monitoring of devices.

c)  Transfer to foreign authorities

The secretly obtained data is passed on to foreign secret services. No worries for all US citizens, this procedure is just a one-way street with German data flowing to your three letter institutions. We jokingly name them "our US backup."

Heribert Prantl, German lawyer, journalist, and author, comments on the strong expansion of security legislation:

"The point is to stop a disastrous development: the legislator dissolves the classic police and criminal law with its very different preconditions in a uniform law of internal security, that no longer distinguishes between guilty and innocent, that no longer knows suspects and non-suspects, but only potential perpetrators who should be monitored for security. Such excess is incompatible with a liberal constitutional state."[21]

But aren't tighter laws better? After all, we must defend our nations against terrorism! Ask yourself, "In times of crisis, what actions a government could classify as "terror." The fuzzy legal terms: "imminent danger" and "potential threat," are to be judged critically in this context. Anyone who sees the topic of "privacy" relaxed and thinks he has nothing to hide, should check out the 9 counterarguments listed on the website of Amnesty International[22].

## Summary

Our history teacher was right. You must have three pillars of democracy and they have to be independent. Power has to be in the hands of different, mutually equal, organs. If this is not the case, established parties will consolidate power and might be tempted to shape democracy to their liking:

- They can decide on the subsidies they receive and the rules restricting them.

- They are mostly unhindered by the controlling bodies and counterweights for which they appoint the most relevant positions.

- The abundant flow of money provides a good basis for their campaign financing.

At the same time, it is possible to speak of a strong expansion of the rights of the executive. This is to be judged very critically because of the potential for massive restrictions of fundamental rights on a very "fuzzy" basis.

---

[21] Translated from: https://www.sueddeutsche.de/politik/sicherheitsgesetze-es-reicht-1.2957958

[22] https://www.amnesty.ca/blog/7-reasons-why-%E2%80%98i%E2%80%99ve-got-nothing-to-hide%E2%80%99-is-the-wrong-response-to-mass-surveillance

## 5. Established parties deciding in their own interest

The established parties are constantly striving to secure and expand their position. To achieve this, they might be tempted to:

- massively expand their own financing
- use their influence to create attractive positions for their protégés and let them act in their best interests
- tweak the electoral situation in their favor
- weaken the very institutions they are controlled by

In all four areas, a lot of established parties are very successful because the system has enabled them to decide "on their own behalf." Representatives are also allowed to decide on the laws and rules that restrict them and their financing and desires to expand. Only a handful of institutions can hold them back with the parties massively influencing the naming for the high ranks for all of these institutions (see Chapter 4).

## 5.1 Party financing

Parties can fund their political work (especially the elections) with public funds or with private money. Incumbent parties can rig the game in their favor.

What happened in Germany and the US?

Germany: In 1967 the parties decided in their own favor, that the state must reimburse them for the "necessary costs of an appropriate election campaign." On the basis of this first decision, the benefices of the parties were then considerably extended over the years. When the party financing was put under public control, the parties found: "substitute instruments for party financing...all well hidden from the public and sealed off from possible controls."[23] While Germany is by far not the only country with public funding,[24] it is certainly in the top range.

"The parliamentary groups in the Bundestag have increased their public financing 35 times between 1968 and 2015: from 4.9 million DM to 83.8 million Euro...Because it had been capped and subject to public control at the end of the 1960s, this increased only 6.7-fold between 1968 and 2015: from 47.3 million Deutsche Mark to 149 million Euro."[25]

The party-related foundations received subsidies totaling 581.4 million euros in 2018.[26]

This and many additional reasons lead to the judgement of Hans Herbert von Arnim:

---

[23] Translated from: Hans Herbert von Arnim, Die Hebel der Macht: und wer sie bedient - Parteienherrschaft statt Volkssouveränität", p. 38

[24] https://en.wikipedia.org/wiki/Party_subsidies

[25] Translated from: Hans Herbert von Arnim, p. 44

[26] Translated from https://www.tagesschau.de/inland/parteinahe-stiftungen-101.html

"We are dealing with a deeply graded abusive overall system that the parties represented in the Bundestag have created themselves, deliberately concealing its multiple unconstitutionality. The secret meaning of the laws passed (or prevented) on their own behalf con-sists in the unhindered procurement of public funds and in their use for their own purposes, excluding extra-parliamentary competitors, as far as possible."[27]

United States: If Germany's democratic powers have no easy time, the democratic powers of the United States have a far tougher one. Here, money has had a decisive political influence for a long time. And this, only increased after the Citizens United vs. FEC case[28] (and a following decision of a lower court) officially sanctioned companies and unions to give unlimited amounts of money to independent political action committees. In the words of most of citizens: "Corruption was legalized." As a result, US politicians spend 30 to 70% of their time calling for dollars instead of focusing on the needs of their constituents.

Aside, American politicians don't have to wait to be chosen by their voters, but instead choose their voters themselves. This is done by defining the congressional voting districts, so that the party's politician has a safe seat. This is called "Gerrymandering." For 2016, it is estimated[29] that The Republicans "won 22 additional U.S. House seats over what would have been expected based on the average vote share in congressional districts across the country." If you want to see some peculiar shapes, take a look at this Wired

---

[27] Translated from: Hans Herbert von Arnim, p. 184

[28] https://en.wikipedia.org/wiki/Citizens_United_v._FEC

[29] https://www.axios.com/gerrymandering-gives-gop-huge-structural-advantage-1513303223-651f6d42-ea5e-4ce4-bda8-ffe9cf6c9e6d.html

article[30]. A very well founded background story on Gerrymandering is given by Dave Galey on the *Another Way Podcast*[31].

American Politicians also indirectly decide *who* can vote. According to iVOTE[32], "51 million Americans are eligible to vote but are not registered, meaning more than 24% of the eligible population is not registered to vote…Those not registered to vote were disproportionately low-income voters, people of color, and younger Americans." And this doesn't count for felons: who have no voting right[33] during incarceration (14 states) or during incarceration and probation (22 states) or even for life (12 states). Voting on a weekday and an over proportional reduction[34] in polling places for minority voter districts add to the picture.

## 5.2 Patronage of public offices

Officially, recruitment and promotion in the public service and the judiciary may only take place according to "personal and material qualification." The party book of applicants may not play a role.

However, the political class also likes to make use of public offices. According to Hans Herbert von Arnim,[35] the office patronage serves:

- the securing of power (patronage of power)

- the reward of partisans (supply patronage)

---

[30] https://www.wired.com/2016/01/gerrymandering-is-even-more-infuriating-when-you-can-actually-see-it/

[31] https://equalcitizens.us/dave-daley-on-gerrymandering/

[32] https://www.ivotecef.org/avr_fact_sheet

[33] http://www.ncsl.org/research/elections-and-campaigns/felon-voting-rights.aspx

[34] https://eu.usatoday.com/story/news/2018/10/30/midterm-elections-closed-voting-sites-impact-minority-voter-turnout/1774221002/

[35] Translated from: Hans Herbert von Arnim, p. 65

- the demonstration of the influence to the outside (demonstration effect)

Every affected person knows what it means to have the right membership book or not to have it. It becomes clear that if you don't belong to the superstars, you should rather join a party in order to get ahead.

The parties especially like to fill positions in their controlling institutions with their own people. These include: high courts, courts of audit, and broadcasting stations. If these are "adequately" staffed, their control is reduced or even largely eliminated. It is no longer possible to speak of a functioning separation of powers.

According to von Arnim, not only high offices in federal and state centers for political education, party foundations, adult education centers, and schools are occupied. Rather, it is a matter of filling millions of lucrative posts:

> "Party book economy impairs equal opportunities, undermines performance in office, inflates the state and administration, endangers their neutrality, presses civil servants into the parties and promotes parties and disenchantment with the state among citizens. Above all, the power orientation of the parties stands in contrast to the factual and value-oriented way of thinking and acting, which is or should be common to the aforementioned institutions; for this very reason they are independent."[36]

> "Those who are only interested in majorities, alliances and the consolidation of their own status and power are in danger of gradually losing the incentive to seek appropriate solutions to problems."[37]

---

[36] Translated from: Hans Herbert von Arnim, p. 67
[37] Translated from: Hans Herbert von Arnim, p. 68

## Summary

The established political parties had the opportunity to rig the political game in their own favor. And they used their chance, to the detriment of democracy.

To a great extent, new parties are disadvantaged by the massive financing given to the incumbent parties. The "party book economy" aligns the state to the interests of the parties and undermines the effectiveness of state institutions. This increases the disenchantment of citizens with parties and the state.

# 6. Influencing the representatives
# in a parliamentary democracy

Lobbying is an often-discussed topic among voters, especially in the United States where lobbying was basically made legal. The *Anti Corruption Act* (which heavily limits lobbying), is supported by 87% of the American people, both progressive and conservative.[38] Even in Germany, where the money flows far less abundant, lobbying is also a topic. 82% of German voters argue for stronger regulations of lobbying.[39]

Representatives of representative democracy can be influenced by interest groups.

Interest groups usually have considerable resources at their disposal to employ lobbyists, publish articles…etc. Thus, economic power leads to political power and causes an overweighting of the interests of these groups in politics.

---

[38] The Strategy to End Corruption: https://youtu.be/UTP4uvIFu5c and Unbreaking America: https://youtu.be/TfQij4aQq1k
[39] Survey results translated from: https://www.abgeordnetenwatch.de/blog/2019-04-24/aktuelle-umfrage-große-mehrheit-will-offenlegung-von-lobbytreffen

"Funders are typically those who have something special to gain from government. Certain industries—telecom, IP—are keen to engage. Others are not. ... , it is the especially interested who spend the most to drive the politics of rent-seeking, the practice of manipulating public policy to increase individual profit."[40]

1.  Distribution of taxpayers' money (subsidies, grants, loans, etc.)
2.  Purchase orders from the public sector
3.  Appointment of persons for positions in state or state-controlled enterprises and organizations
4.  Setting up obstacles for new competitors (laws, directives, regulations)
5.  Creating a favorable legal framework

Enterprises and business organizations tend to exploit the regulatory scope of influence to obtain the benefits listed above. Moral considerations are not part of the market economy equation whose goal is to maximize profits. If the "investment" in another lobbyist promises more profit than an investment in a new innovation, then the decision becomes obvious.

In a system of separated powers, you can stop things much more easily than you can make them happen. Incumbents that benefit from the established extractive rules, have an easy time to block initiatives that challenge the status quo.

Montana Governor and presidential candidate Steve Bullock:

"When you look at climate, income inequality, drug prices, gun safety, so many of these things can be tracked back to the lack of action

---

[40] Lawrence Lessig, They Don't Represent Us: Reclaiming Our Democracy, Position 1092

really as a corrupting influence of money in the system." .. "So it's not even the spending of money, it's just knowing that this money could be spend if a senator or representative steps out of line."[41]

## 6.1 How many lobbyists are there?

Washington and Brussels are the top lobby epicenters of the world. About 6,000 lobbyists are active in Berlin.[42] The estimation of *Lobbypedia* lists about 30,000 lobbyists at EU level.[43] In Washington D.C., there are about 11,650 lobbyists. [44] According to the analyst James Thurber, this figure goes up to about 100,000 when you include the shadow lobbyists[45]. The interview[46] of "The Empire Files" with US Congressional researcher James D'Angelo, is a great way to understand the mechanisms of lobbying in the US.

So, let us assume that the average German lobbyist, including side costs, costs a low estimate of 166,000 euro per year. That would be 1 billion euros alone for Berlin. To be fair, you need to include the costs for employees dealing with the topic in the corporate headquarters and those of external experts whom need to be consulted for the drafting of bills. Spending on party donations and direct donations are also not accounted for.

If you take the numbers from *opensecrets.org* you can calculate an average expense per lobbyist in Washington D.C. of close to $300,000 with a total of $3.46 billion for the official lobbyists. According to the Sunlight Founda-

---

[41] https://equalcitizens.us/gov-steve-bullock-on-getting-big-money-out-of-politics/ min 22:20 and 23:50

[42] Translated from: https://www.berliner-zeitung.de/berlin/politikberater-in-berlin-arbeiten-etwa-6000-lobbyisten-30141618

[43] https://lobbypedia.de/wiki/Portal_Lobbyismus_in_der_EU

[44] https://www.opensecrets.org/lobby/

[45] https://www.thenation.com/article/shadow-lobbying-complex/

[46] https://www.youtube.com/watch?v=c4kvUxQIJlA

tion[47], the estimations for registered and stealth lobbying were about $6.7 billion for 2012.

For companies and other communities of interest, lobbyists are an investment. This is only done as the client expects that he will get more out than he invests. In other words, it is safe to consider that there are billions to be made by influencing Berlin and many more by influencing Brussels and Washington. A research[48] showed that in one instance, US lobbyists brought in $220 for every dollar spent on them.

## 6.2 How can lobbyists influence elected representatives?

The following considerations of potential possibilities of influencing are, of course, purely theoretical considerations. I assume that representatives will resist all temptation and will not be influenced. However, I also assume that they must be supported by appropriate regulations and controls in their efforts.

Contributions to parties or campaigns

- Direct donations to the party or a campaign
- Indirect donations to the party through middlemen
- Overpriced ads in the parties' publications
- Overpriced stand fee at party conferences
- Donate to the affiliated foundations
- …

---

[47] https://sunlightfoundation.com/2013/11/25/how-much-lobbying-is-there-in-washington-its-double-what-you-think/
[48] https://papers.ssrn.com/sol3/papers.cfm?abstract_id=1375082

Grants to parliamentarians

- Direct donations to the re-election campaign of politicians, increasing the chances that only the "right" candidates are elected
- Good positions in business or in lobby organizations, business-related foundations, or think tanks, etc.
- Excessive speaking fees
- Excessive consulting fees
- High upfront payments for memoirs of parliamentarians
- ...

Indirect contributions to representatives

- Placing orders to companies belonging to a parliamentarian (or, his brother-in-law)
- Admission of children to a popular kindergarten
- Admission of a child to an elite university
- Early promotion of a child in his job or an attractive offer from a new employer
- Donation to a charitable cause affiliated with the parliamentarian
- ...

Blackmail and intimidation

- Blackmail based on secrets that the representative would not like the public to see
- Threat of a "smear campaign" against the representative
- Threat of massive support for a rival candidate during the next election
- ...

As Transparency International found out "30% of MEPs who have left politics now work for organizations on the EU lobby register. For European Commissioners, the share is more than 50%."[49]

In 2013 a PowerPoint presentation to incoming freshmen by the Democratic Congressional Campaign Committee was leaked to the Huffington Post. This paper recommended to spend four out of nine active hours of their time as 'call time' calling in money for their re-election campaign.[50]

According to Vox[51], half of retiring US senators and a third of retiring House members register as lobbyists. The graph displayed in the article, showing the percentage of retirees registering as lobbyists, vividly reveals the sellout of US democracy. The reason is simple. According to a video[52] from RepresentUs, the average raise for the new lobbyists is 1452%.

U.S. Senator and presidential candidate Michael Bennet said in an interview:[53]

> "You wanna know why Congress can't get anything done in the works of Citizens United? It's because politicians are fearful that if they do something, let's say have a floor speech on climate or join a bill on climate, that the billionaires will say: 'Well, if you are gonna do that, we are gonna spend thirty million dollars in your primary election.' And then everybody backs of. And over the ten-year period that I have been there you know you don't have to see the money to know that it is there. They don't even have to spend the money they threatened wit. And that's why

---

[49] https://transparency.eu/wp-content/uploads/2017/01/Access-all-areas.pdf
[50] https://www.huffpost.com/entry/call-time-congressional-fundraising_n_2427291
[51] https://www.vox.com/2016/1/15/10775788/revolving-door-lobbying
[52] https://www.youtube.com/watch?v=b4jdcdlquF0&feature=youtu.be
[53] https://equalcitizens.us/day-one-campaign-finance-reform-senator-michael-bennet-on-unclogging-a-corrupt-congress/ min 15:09-

it becomes a corruption of inaction."

The results of the gridlock caused by the inaction are described by Gehl and Porter:[54]

> "Today, however, our political system has become the major barrier to solving nearly every important challenge our nation needs to address."

This list of potential influences is not exhaustive. The ingenuity of lobbyists and interest groups behind them is unlimited. We can only state that there are many ways to reward parties and representatives who are playing along. There are also many ways to punish those who do not. Many of these rewards and punishments are extremely hard to trace.

As Lawrence Lessig pointed out in his book *They don't Represent Us* it is not only about direct bribes:[55]

> "Instead, this bending in Washington comes through the subtle nudge of perpetual fundraising, tied to the cuddling and collaboration with lobbyists. Persuasion is through favor, not bribe. It comes through obliging someone, not from purchasing them."

## 6.3 Who will lobbyists try to influence?

The task of the lobbyists is to influence the government's decisions. The interest group represented by them should be adequately taken into account in the decisions or even better given preferential treatment. In order to be able to achieve this goal optimally, efforts should be targeted to achieve the highest level of efficiency.

---

[54] https://gehlporter.com/part-i-setting-the-stage/
[55] Lawrence Lessig, They Don't Represent Us: Reclaiming Our Democracy, Position 1092

## OPTION A

The lobbyists could meet with all representatives and try to convince them of the correctness of their arguments. If this does not work, they could bribe them, so that they vote in their favor.

EFFORT: High, most parliaments have hundreds of members. That would be a considerable amount of time and money.

YIELD: Low, as most individual representatives don't have a "say" in decisions (see Chapter 1).

RISK: The risk of discovery increases with broad-based bribery/influence campaigns, as the number of potential vulnerabilities increases.

## OPTION B

The lobbyists could only meet with the leaders of the parties. They talk intensively to the members of the ruling party/governing coalition, as they can direct/make decisions in this legislative period.

EFFORT: Low, as there are very few people.

CHALLENGE: It is difficult to meet with these people because all interest groups want to talk to them.

EARNING: High, since many decisions are prepared or made here.

RISK: Low, because in case of doubt, only a few people need to be influenced.

## OPTION C

The lobbyists could meet with the members of the committees who prepare decision-making or even legislative proposals on individual topics.

EFFORT: Medium, since it is only a limited number of persons.

CHALLENGE: It is not easy to talk to these people because all groups interested in the committee's issues want to speak to them.

EARNING: High, since many decisions are prepared or elaborated here.

RISK: Middle, since in case of doubt only a few people have to be influenced.

In practice, the lobbyists will try to utilize all possibilities of the influencing strategies, especially B and C. These will most likely achieve the greatest impact for time and monetary units spent. In the sense of a long-term strategy however, investments will also be made in the "simple representative." After all, they could eventually become leaders or be appointed to committees or influence decision-makers or can be the deciding vote. Real-life lobbyism doesn't stop there. Employees of representatives will be also included.

According to representative John Sarbanes the "money people" will contact you even before you are sworn in as member of the congress to gain access and influence.[56]

## 6.4 Are lobbyists generally to be rejected?

As described in the first chapter, politicians have many issues and must decide on them. For most of these topics, they need to get detailed input in advance to form a well-informed opinion. So, if representatives take their job seriously, it is imperative that they educate themselves about the topics.

It makes sense to bundle this information in a collection. After all, it does not make much sense for 100 representatives to independently read about 100 new topics. They simply have no time. In this respect, central preparation is more efficient.

---

[56] https://equalcitizens.us/the-author-of-hr-1-on-the-for-the-people-act/, listen from min 10

In this central preparation of the topics however, extreme attention must be paid to a correct representation of the situation, the basic problem, the options for action, and expected outcomes. This must be created to the best of knowledge and must be absolutely neutral. Building on this, the respective party should then make a value-based recommendation to their representatives.

It is quite legitimate and almost inevitable to obtain information and opinions on the individual topic areas. But representatives should keep in mind that information from lobbyists, i.e. representatives of associations, companies, foundations, NGOs,…etc., should all be treated with caution. They have their own agenda.

The representatives, who are responsible for the preparation, should use their time optimally. They should aim at the highest possible information gain. It is very unlikely that this can be achieved if representatives to 90% only talk to company representatives.

In a true democracy, mandatory registers with accredited lobbyists are indispensable. The information has to include: the budget, the information on whose behalf it influences policy, and the relevant subject areas. Rules must define clear identification points when someone has to be officially registered and classified as a lobbyist.

A list of meetings with lobbyists should also be kept. In this directory, the attendees should be noted as well as: the subject, the time, and the duration of the meeting. This could be done very easily via a selective readout of the parliamentary calendars compiling marked entries. In order to be able to evaluate meetings with lobbyists automatically, the following procedure should be followed:

- All lobbyists must register officially

- The list of lobbyists is offered in the calendar by drop down selection
- The logging of meetings with lobbyists are mandatory
- Representatives are only allowed to meet with officially registered lobbyists

Registering as a lobbyist should be easy. There should be very few hurdles. After all, it is not a representative not meeting with lobbyists, but of gaining transparency about their meetings.

This openness applies only to the exchange of arguments for a decision. It does not apply to money or other benefits. Money distorts a neutral view and the fair representation of voters. Monetary contributions from companies or organizations to members of parliament, political parties, or candidates should be forbidden.

The current situation in America is different from this ideal. A graphic by RepresentUs, in their video "Corruption is legal in America"[57], explains very well, how politicians align with the top 10% and their money. America needs laws to ban lobbyists from coordinating fundraisers. Close the revolving door and ban shadow lobbying. This is already on the way, as part of the *AntiCorruptionAct.org*. Supported by 87% of the American people, progressive and conservative, it aims to be passed as law city by city and state by state all the way to the federal level.[58] Another bill is the *People Act from 2019*, also called HR1, that tackles problems with voting, political money, redistricting and ethics.[59]

---

[57] https://www.youtube.com/watch?v=5tu32CCA_Ig&feature=youtu.be&t=136
[58] The Strategy to End Corruption, https://youtu.be/UTP4uvIFu5c
[59] https://en.wikipedia.org/wiki/For_the_People_Act_of_2019 and
https://www.npr.org/2019/01/05/682286587/house-democrats-introduce-anti-corruption-bill-as-symbolic-first-act?t=1568896044162

## Summary

Lobbying is a legitimate way to influence politics. However, in order to ensure democratic control, mechanisms must be established to ensure that representatives get a balanced view of the issue.

The time spent by representatives with lobbyists of diverse interest groups are a good indicator for a balanced information gathering. A mandatory lobby register is a must. A list of meetings with lobbyists is also to be introduced.

Lobbying should be restricted to give good reasons for a decision, but not money.

# 7. Influencing voters in a direct democracy

I recommend reading *The Dictators Handbook*, which describes the connection between the size of the group to be influenced and corruption. As the size of the group grows, so does the level of corruption shrink.[60] Another more entertaining way to learn about the topic is in a 20 minute video titled *"The Rules for Rulers"*[61].

According to this approach, extending the group size to be influenced to the entire electorate would be the optimal strategy to combat corruption. In other words, the introduction of direct democracy would be the optimal strategy against corruption.

Is it conceivable that individual voters can be bribed? Or voter groups? Or that voters can be indirectly influenced?

---

[60] Bruce Bueno de Mescita, The Dictator's Handbook, p. 281
[61] https://www.youtube.com/watch?v=rStL7niR7gs

## 7.1 Direct Bribery of Individual Voters

The direct bribery of individual voters would be very uneconomical. On one hand, it is very expensive to find out what the individual voter wants to negotiate with him. On the other hand, there is not enough to distribute to buy a large number of votes.

But if it would be easier? The parties or interest groups interested in the election of the party do not have to conduct complicated negotiations. They could simply buy votes.

Is that possible?

Today's voting systems make this difficult. After all, the bribed voter must be able to demonstrate credibly that he has chosen the "right" party. But how? The voter is handed the ballot paper in the polling station. Then he has to make his choice and put it in the ballot box. He has no proof who he has chosen.

How can this be avoided to provide credible proof?

- The election fraudster could organize a blank ballot paper and fill this in with his choices. He could then hand it to a voter. The voter has to stick this into the ballot box and return the ballot paper he was handed by the election officials to the fraudster.

- The bribed voter could use a video live stream of his ballot to prove that he has chosen "correctly."

- The bribed voter could apply for absentee voting and complete the whole process at home. The "election helper" could even come to his house and fill out the ballot paper there. Or the voter could open the envelope, sign the statement of correctness, and send it to the "electoral helper" together with the ballot envelope and the blank ballot paper.

The third option is less expensive and promises good potential. In 2017, the proportion of postal voting participants rose steadily and reached 18% in Great Britain[62] and 28.6% in Germany.[63] The US number was 40.8% for the 2016[64] presidential election, even though absentee voting requires an excuse in 19 states.[65]

In reality, all of these fraud types are very dangerous. A secret known by many people know is none. The single bribed voter could earn far more money by giving an exclusive interview to a newspaper.

Overall, this direct bribery of voters is therefore very unlikely.

## 7.2 Further influences on the individual voter

Citizens have personal and group interests and are influenced by them in their choice.

Financial interests:

- A citizen on welfare benefits will tend to choose a party that promises to increase welfare rates or reduce sanctions.
- A citizen on welfare benefits will more likely choose a party that is committed to introducing an unconditional basic income.
- A family is more likely to choose a party that promises to raise child benefits.

---

[62] https://www.electoralcommission.org.uk/__data/assets/pdf_file/0004/234976/UKPGE-2017-electoral-data-report.pdf

[63] https://www.bundeswahlleiter.de/info/presse/mitteilungen/bundestagswahl-2017/35_17_briefwaehler.html

[64] https://www.eac.gov/documents/2017/10/17/eavs-deep-dive-early-absentee-and-mail-voting-data-statutory-overview/

[65] http://www.ncsl.org/research/elections-and-campaigns/absentee-and-early-voting.aspx

- An artist whose projects are mainly state-funded will be more likely to choose a party that is committed to handing out these specific subsidies.

- ...

This does not mean that each individual of these groups will elect the parties that make promises in their favor. It just means that the voters of these groups will tend towards these parties and statistically disproportionately vote for them.

Of course, it also depends on the underlying value system of the party. What it stands for, the past of the party and what it has already done and what not. In the context of the party's past, the credibility of campaign promises is also important. If the party has already broken many promises, and the voters consider the promises to be "hot air," they will not be influenced by them. This is especially true if the breach of trust was obvious and happened only recently.

The voter's own value system also determines the choice he makes. He will not choose "what he is not." He will choose a party whose general orientation he can identify with:

- left vs. right

- central vs. decentral

- liberal "Leave us alone!" vs. the nanny state "Take care of us all!"

- multicultural vs. "foreigners out"

- military missions vs. no missions abroad

- security vs. informational self-determination

- ...

## 7.3 Influence by interest groups

In order to claim state subsidies, it is helpful to present your group as weak or disadvantaged or discriminated against. This not only increases the chances of money for the group, but also gives the state an argument to justify its existence. It also justifies the distribution of these benefits in the name of "social justice."

Some groups go far beyond wanting to achieve equality. They do not demand rights that apply to everyone. They want privileges that apply only to their group, which can only be granted to them when others are forced to "pay" for it. Examples include quotas or anti-discrimination laws that restrict freedom of speech.

Some of these groups, e.g. in France, the public service or the farmers, are very outspoken. They are fast to march on the streets, if their rights and/or privileges are threatened.

Very often, as with the above three examples, there are tangible economic interests behind these pressure groups. In this respect, they are a very effective concentration of individual economic interests and their representation. Further interests may also be in the foreground or play a further role.

The negative side effect of these disproportionately influencing pressure groups is a misjudged policy-making process:

- Voters who organize themselves effectively in groups are given preferential treatment.
- The groups that are most outspoken and persistent are the ones most likely to be "served."

It is very likely that there will be a misallocation of public money. Socially meaningful changes can be massively delayed.

## 7.4 Influence by statistics

Quantitative research and statistics are indispensable tools in order to be able - independent of the subjective perception - to show the systematics of tendencies and contexts in various areas of life.

In a positive sense, statistics could be used as the basis for evidence-based policy decisions, such as those proposed by the Evidence Initiative[66].

However, government commissioned statistics seem to also serve other purposes such as:

a)  leaving the public unaware of the true extent of a situation and

b)  glossing over negative developments during a party's term or reinforcing positive developments.

One might even speak of deliberate deception when the naming for the statistic is so misleading that the understanding of the average voter is too far away from the official statistical results.

A favorite is the unemployment statistics:

United States of America

The United States has about twice the real unemployment rate as the official rate shows. This is because the official rate only counts workers still in the labor force who must have looked for a job in the last four weeks. If you count in these marginally attached and add the underemployed workers that work part-time but would prefer to work full-time, you receive the actual

---

[66] https://evidenceinitiative.economist.com/

unemployment rate. For May 2019, the official unemployment rate was 3.6%, yet the real unemployment rate was 7.1%.[67]

## International Labor Office

Most of the countries use data on unemployment as defined by the International Labor Office (ILO). This solely includes permanent residents who are out of work, looking for a job, and could start working within a short time. A worker who only works one hour a week is not considered unemployed. Consider this if you hear about high unemployment rates. The truth is, the actual rates are even more shocking.

## Germany

The counting method for unemployment is defined by laws. The parties have repeatedly corrected the definition of the number of unemployed and lowered the official count. At present, close to one million people are not included in the unemployment statistics. They "are participating in programs of active labor market policy or are temporarily ill or older than 58 years and receive welfare (Hartz IV)."[68] The official unemployment rate is 4.8% and the underemployment rate is 6.9%. The German statistics can still be described as relatively fair. It still counts low-paid workers (less than 15 hours per week) as unemployed.[69]

---

[67] https://www.thebalance.com/what-is-the-real-unemployment-rate-3306198
[68] http://www.spiegel.de/wirtschaft/soziales/arbeitslosenstatistik-so-hoch-ist-die-verdeckte-arbeitslosigkeit-a-1133354.html
[69] Translated from: https://statistik.arbeitsagentur.de/Statischer-Content/Unterbeschaeftigung-Schaubild.pdf

## 7.5 Influence by media

The media plays a central role in democracy. In a truly democratic state, it should oversee and criticize the legislature, the judiciary, and the executive as the "fourth power in the state." Media is the early warning system and the safety net of democracy.

The job of a political journalist is not that of the stenographer. His job is rather to inform the public about what influential people and institutions do with their money and on their behalf.

The intellectual Noam Chomsky put it this way:

> "A truly independent press rejects the role of subordination to power and authority. It casts the orthodoxy to the winds, questions what 'right-thinking people will accept without question,' tears aside the veil of tacit censorship, makes available to the general public the information and range of opinions and ideas that are a prerequisite for meaningful participation in social and political life, and beyond that, offers a platform for people to enter into debate and discussion about the issues that concern them. By doing so it serves its function as a foundation for a truly free and democratic society."[70]

The reality in many countries, however, is different and the media is far closer to the government than it should be. Some of the media are even controlled directly by parties. Most are in the hands of a few wealthy individuals.

> "Freedom of press is the freedom of two hundred rich persons
> to spread their view."
> Paul Sethe, German Publicist

---

[70] https://chomsky.info/01072017/

Too often a clean journalistic separation of facts and opinion is omitted. Facts are not researched or, even deliberately left aside. A current example is the UN migration pact. Exaggerated ethics and fast at hand public blaming prevent urgently needed open discussions.

Only a minority of citizens additionally informs itself via alternative media which offers a different perspective to state or mainstream media. Many people have no time for this. Most of them also have no interest in it. They remain in their own filter bubble, especially as a result of the mechanisms of social media.

But why is it so important?

We are continually bombarded with millions of impressions. Only a few can be consciously processed by our brains. Our brain chooses shortcuts as it doesn't want to be unnecessarily burdened. These shortcuts are controlled by stereotypes or "pictures" that help us to make fast "standard decisions."

In our complex world we develop images of people and things we have never encountered personally in life. These are largely taken from the media. By consuming the same media, these images are consolidated through repetition and form the basis of our decisions and actions. Only rarely do we question those.

As described before interest groups will try to influence the public opinion. In his book *Solving For Democracy* Tony Bracks describes the three-step process of well-funded organizations as follows:

> "The first phase required an 'investment' in intellectuals whose ideas would serve as the 'raw products'. The second required an investment in think tanks that would turn the ideas into marketable policies. And the third phase required the subsidization of 'citizens'

groups that would, along with 'special interests', pressure elected officials to implement the policies."

On the other side there is no such thing as absolute objective journalism. Journalists always have to pick the parts they want to feature and thus select. Media does not describe reality but (at least partly) creates it.

A larger part of media doesn't inform people objectively, so that they can form their own view. Instead most media try to form the opinion by spreading their "pictures." Complex topics are unilaterally defined by the framing set by the media reports and predefined terms and pictures. A judgmental ethic attempts to limit the field of discussion and prevent discussions about facts and opinions that go beyond the defined field. Urgently necessary discussions are prevented.

## A. Long-term opinion forming

In marketing it is a well-known fact that the customer must have multiple contact with a product before buying it. This also applies to the sale of political messages and "truths." The more often one repeats these, the longer they are uncontested, the higher is the probability that the voter will believe them, or that they will successfully sow doubts.

This "truth" is achieved by defining or hiding topics, setting frameworks, defining terms, selective reporting, selective selection of experts, and discrediting dissenters.

According to Noam Chomsky, the propagandist does not want to convince, but to influence the emotions and behavior of people. He wants to frighten them, make them angry. He gives promises to them. Propaganda tries to replace self-sovereign thinking with the gut feeling of "being right" with the accepted opinion.

In the long-term, work repetition is key. Professor Mausfeld, German professor for psychology: "A number of experimental studies show that an assertion made by the experimenters increases in the perceived truth of the observers the more frequently they are presented. This is even true if the experimenter explicitly declared them false before the experiment. We are unable to fight it. Even if you clarify the phenomenon beforehand with the test subject, it does not change the effect: the more often you hear an opinion, the more the perceived truth increases." [71]

> "In fact, you just have to repeat a lie constantly and in different TV programs and newspapers, then it is often believed."
> -Daniele Ganser, Swiss Historian and Peace Scientist

a) Set or hide topics

The hardest type of selection is the positive selection. It limits to only what the definition contains. If the mainstream media only reports on allowed topics, other topics are not public. These other topics are largely hidden. Only a few politically interested individuals obtain additional information via alternative media.

Example: The current war in Yemen is euphemistically labeled "military intervention" in Wikipedia. According to international law, it is an illegal war. And it is rarely reported upon by the media. The war has created the biggest supply crisis in the world and has led to a dramatic outbreak of cholera.

---

[71] Translated from: Rainer Mausfeld, Warum schweigen die Lämmer?: Wie Elitendemokratie und Neoliberalismus unsere Gesellschaft und unsere Lebensgrundlagen bedrohen, Position 519

b) Set terms and their interpretation

The race for the mind of the public is already won at an early stage by setting the frame and asking questions. If you accept the question, you are already in the construct of the person posing the questions.

Topics can be very unilaterally defined by deliberately chosen one-sided terms spread via media. If you are able to define the terms, you have already gained half of the authority to interpret the topic.

> "Peacekeeping:" The victim does not care if the bombs that falls on him belong to a war or peace-keeping mission. It does not matter to him whether the previous surveillance that led to the bombing was part of a war or a peace-keeping mission.
>
> "Refugees:" "What unites all these people is their hope - or smartphone-driven illusion - for a better life in rich Europe. The reasons for leaving home are often completely different. And a not inconsiderable part will not be recognized as a refugee in the end. So why are all (German) politicians and (German) press using the label 'refugees'? Why is one so scared to call the current migration 'immigration'? The legally correct term 'illegal border crossing' is avoided as far as possible." [72]

The choice of words directs the thoughts that arise when the word is pronounced:

> warn vs. threaten
>
> freedom fighter vs. terrorist
>
> resistance vs. terror
>
> peace mission vs. war

---

[72] Translated from Süddeutsche Zeitung "Geflüchtete: Streit ums Wort"

military strike vs. war of aggression

c) Selective reporting

Selective reporting skips listing important facts that are relevant for assessing the situation. It only selects the facts that match its own agenda.

> Example 1: Reporting on the Ukraine conflict and the image of the "evil Russian"
>
> Facts left out: Expansion of NATO as threat to Russia, background of the seizure of power in Ukraine, shots on police and civilians on the Maidan.[73]
>
> Example 2: As you can easily research, today's coverage of Venezuela is also very one-sided and international opinion much less unanimous than reported.[74]

Journalist and author Ulrich Tilgner: "The media do not lie - they shorten, hide, distort and tamper. However, I react allergic to the word 'lying press'. Because this presupposes a conscious act. Exactly these are rare in the media. Rather, the employees there have their own perception of an increasingly complex reality, of which they then show excerpts. They assume official political positions or of those their employers. In order to avoid contradictions, they resort to the means of shortening - not least because they believe that this shortening facilitates the understanding of the public."[75]

---

[73] Translated from: https://www.heise.de/tp/features/Maidanmorde-Drei-Beteiligte-gestehen-3893551.html?seite=all

[74] https://youtu.be/ii5MlQgGXyk, Empire Files Episode 79 - An Ocean of Lies on Venezuela: Abby Martin & UN Rapporteur Expose Coup

[75] Translated from: Jens Wernicke, Lügen die Medien? Propaganda, Rudeljournalismus und der Kampf um die öffentliche Meinung, p. 70, Ulrich Tilgner

Stephen Hebel adds: "They do not invent the 'good might stories' but they pass them on. The inventors are located elsewhere: in business associations, in the policy and PR departments of political parties, in foundations such as Bertelsmann or in more or less covert propaganda departments such as the Institute for German Business or the initiative New Social Market Economy financed by the metal association."[76]

## d) Selective selection of experts

Experts who are very relevant to the press because of their position and their knowledge are not contacted any more. Example: Willi Wimmer, who was OSCE vice-president in the period before the Yugoslav war. After he had made a critical comment against Germany joining the war, he was no longer "in media demand," as his opinion contradicted the desired direction.

## e) Discrediting persons

A particularly perfidious way of combating other opinions is to put the opponents in the moral off and give them names like "monster" or "Nazi" or simply "un-patriotic." In extreme cases, this can take on a totalitarian character and end in a career and even life-threatening character assassination.

These persons can be denied the right to express their arguments, thus preventing a factual debate.

## f) Talk shows

In talk shows, three to six guests are invited to discuss a complex topic. But as described under d), it is not necessary to invite people who are well

---

[76] Translated from: Jens Wernicke, p. 80, Stephan Hebel

informed and who are able to represent their opinion in a well-founded and convincing way.

Even if a real expert is invited, he is only a single participant in the round. Often, he can only give his intro statement, has a few minutes in the middle, and his closing statement. The topic of discussion is rarely embedded in the larger context. The underlying mechanisms are only touched upon and solutions are only described superficially.

In short: the talk show only pretends to present and discuss a topic. The scope of the discussion, however, is set so that the topic must remain on the surface. What remains is a confused citizen who only knows that the subject is complicated and tedious. This suggests that he would be better off to leave this topic to the professionals, the politicians.

B. Directing opinions in the days directly before the election

Many voters have no firm opinion on a topic. The two extremes are the complete lack of interest in a topic and the complex balancing of both sides:

- Voter Type A: "The topic does not interest me at all. I have no opinion"

  versus

- Voter Type B: "I've educated myself about both sides. I can understand both sides. I do not know yet how I will decide."

In order to activate Voter Type A for elections and win both undecided for a political party, it is advisable to activate the voter through an event shortly before the election. Voter Type A quickly forms an opinion and Voter Type B gets the final kick to take the "right" decision.

An event shortly before the election has the strongest effect. A new discovery about a previous event might also work. The weakest, but still very helpful, would be a one-sided compilation of old events.

Anyone who has seen some agent thrillers can easily imagine how these election-influencing events can be fabricated as needed on a timely basis. If you want to orientate yourself on the sometimes no less exciting reality, take a look at (historically proven) lies that have led to wars.

C. Social Media - The Echo Chamber

The algorithms of the social media platforms serve their users personalized information. They aim to keep them on their platform and earn more money from advertisers.

The user gets into a self-created and algorithm created filter bubble, which enhances his own views and hides other ideas and world views. The algorithms of the platforms appeal to our human instincts. It attempts to motivate us to stay as long as possible by means of targeted, individualized display of content. This is often achieved by feeding "…us a constant stream of increasingly more extreme and inflammatory content".[77]

This often leads to little questioning of one's own worldview. If the user stumbles upon other ideas, they seem even more incomprehensible or even threatening. One of the reactions is "hate speech." The use of classic social media reinforces the further polarization of society,[78] as seen in the Brexit

---

[77] http://humanetech.com/wp-content/uploads/2019/07/CHT-Undivided-Attention-Podcast-Ep.4-Down-the-Rabbit-Hole.pdf, p. 6
[78] https://samharris.org/podcasts/152-trouble-facebook/

case.[79] Individuals are rather oriented along identity politics, build their own tribes, focus on differences and miss to align along common interests.

If you are unlucky, foreign intelligence agencies buy ads and influence the election. This can also be done by other organizations that have money and want their interests represented.

In the future, the situation is more likely to worsen. "Deep Fakes" are increasingly used to simulate realities that never existed. Imagine what a deceptively genuine, but fake video of a politician could cause. Slander and manipulation become easier. It will also become easier to deny statements actually made as "deep fake."[80] A phenomenon that law professors Robert Chesney and Danielle Citron described as "liar's dividend."

## Summary

Buying votes is technically feasible, but due to the high administrative burden and the risk of discovery, unsuitable. The most visible bribes are election promises, which are used to win interest groups and votes.

The influence of misleading statistics and media is much subtler. Topics are set or excluded in the mainstream media, terms and concepts are defined. The selective choice of experts and facts creates a clear or complicated picture, as required by the current political will. Social media is an amplifier. Controlled by the revenue-oriented mechanisms, the user enters an echo

---

[79] https://www.ted.com/talks/carole_cadwalladr_facebook_s_role_in_brexit_and_the_threat_to_democracy#t-49559

[80] https://medium.com/thewashingtonpost/top-ai-researchers-race-to-detect-deepfake-videos-we-are-outgunned-ce4c057b0625 and
https://twimlai.com/twiml-talk-260-fighting-fake-news-and-deep-fakes-with-machine-learning-w-delip-rao/ starting from min. 30:29

chamber. This connects him with like-minded users and strengthens his opinion. The polarization of society increases.

# 8. Can the citizen be entrusted with this power?

What happens when citizens themselves can propose and vote on legislative changes?

Can we entrust this responsibility and power to the citizen?

## 8.1 Fears of the critics

Opponents of direct democracy paint a bleak picture. In a global world, political systems are so complex that they can hardly be reduced to a simple "yes" or "no". People's opinion would become the playground of influential media houses and interest groups. These can invest a lot of money in their influencing campaigns. Even worse, the masses can be influenced by populists or even demagogues. Fear and resistance are easier to mobilize than enthusiasm.

The opponents assume that soon the death penalty will be reintroduced. Democratic rights will get restricted or abolished (at least for certain parts of society). Many new benefits would be introduced that would be impossible to finance or which would unduly burden future generations.

"When the people find that they can vote themselves money that will herald the end of the republic."

-Benjamin Franklin

An example often cited as one of these wrong decisions is the "minaret referendum" in Switzerland in 2007. The voters decided to add a passage to the Swiss Constitution, that bans building for minarets. The initiative was accepted with 57.5% of the voters and 19.5 out of 26 of the Swiss stands. The voter turnout was 53.4%[81].

One can argue about the result of this Swiss vote. But the voters were actually asked to decide, and did so after a broad discussion in society. Switzerland itself is a successful model of direct democracy. Around three quarters[82] of Swiss citizens go to the polls more or less regularly. According to empirical studies, despite increasingly complex issues, the majority of the electorate is predominantly well informed about voting issues.[83]

In order to avoid spontaneous reactions that lead to ill-considered and poorly thought-out decisions, the Swiss system has clearly defined timetables. These or similar mechanisms need to be built into a system. These prevent short-term decisions and give voters time to be fully informed about the issue (see Chapter 13.1).

Anyone who has ever dealt with the strengths and weaknesses of our thinking knows that we humans have two kinds of thinking. This is described by the Nobel Prize winner for economics, Daniel Kahneman, in his book *Thinking, Fast and Slow*. The book states, during evolution humans developed a strategy

---

[81] https://www.bk.admin.ch/ch/d/pore/va/20091129/index.html

[82] https://www.nzz.ch/schweiz/politische-beteiligung-in-der-schweiz-wird-unterschaetzt-1.18121101

[83] Translated from: http://www.politan.ch/wie-informiert-ist-das-schweizer-stimmvolk-uber-die-ihm-vorgelegten-sachfragen/

in which most of the decisions of the day are made without much thinking. We just use proven shortcuts. This "fast thinking," is however very susceptible and is subject to many cognitive biases[84] which can be used for manipulation. In political decision-making, the most important thing is not to let the voter decide "from the gut." He must know the facts and be motivated to deal with them. Then he has a good basis for his decision.

## 8.2 US investigation disproves the fears of critics

Politics professor Elizabeth Gerber published a study in 1999. She explores the question if those whom win in a referendum spend the most money on advertising and propaganda or own the media. She investigated 100 referendums from eight US states.

The study found citizens-supported initiatives had a much greater chance of success than those promoted by business associations. In other words, the fear of critics of direct democracy that certain wealthy interest groups would dominate legislation has been rejected by the study.

Citizens' initiatives have been far more successful than lobbyists, particularly in the fight for new laws. The lobbyists have therefore, quite successfully, focused on hinder citizens' reform initiatives. Here, the amount of campaign spending plays an important role.

Professor Hermann Heußner, who has researched direct democracy, assesses the situation in the US as follows:

> "Overall, there are no indications that financially strong circles have been able to manipulate the people in such a way that they managed to pass laws whose results were rejected by the majority of the

---

[84] https://en.wikipedia.org/wiki/List_of_cognitive_biases

people. Business associations therefore usually prefer lobbying in parliaments. Here the influence is more effective, cheaper and more independent of public opinion."[85]

## 8.3 Encouraging experiences with new participatory models

Democracy tends to work poorly when individuals solely reach a judgement on their own. If individuals do not feel the need to articulate their ideas and to test, and if necessary, correct them by exchanging them with others, there is no deliberation, but just a vote. But, only the view out of one's own filter bubble and a discourse can lead to an increase in knowledge about the respective topic, its mechanisms, and an understanding of the positions of others.

But who has the time to inform himself intensively about all political topics and to form a well-founded opinion on them? This is the only convincing argument a representation by a smaller group of delegates who represent the electorate as a whole and make decisions for it. This group can focus fully on the issues and will therefore be able to achieve better thought-out results.

Most of us only know parliamentary democracy with its parties and their professional politicians as their representatives. Historically however, there are other models that have been very successful. Particularly, the allocation of a large proportion of public offices by lot. This type of democratic representation was e.g. practiced in Athens and during the Renaissance in the city-states of Venice and Florence.

---

[85] Translated from: Hermann Heußner, Mehr direkte Demokratie wagen!, p. 135 und 136

Mini publics as a representation of the population

In the last two decades, the use of these models has led to many positive experiences worldwide. So-called "mini-publics," have been used to discuss complex problems and propose solutions. The participants of these groups, who are to represent the public, are drawn by lot according to their characteristics (age, gender, educational level,...etc.). They form a smaller representative picture of the population. If one citizen refuses to participate in the group, the next citizen with similar characteristics will be drawn.

In the processes the group is supported by professional facilitators. The information required for assessment is obtained by citizens through hearing and consultation of experts and representatives of all relevant stakeholders. These are not present during the evaluation work. The results of the group's consultations are summarized in a citizens' report. This is made available to the political decision-making bodies as a consultation document.

The mini publics are primarily intended to provide a sheltered space. A limited number of citizens receive balanced information. Deliberative discussions with fellow citizens from different social groups are encouraged. This is mainly achieved by:

a)   the selection of participants that represents a representative cross-section of the population and enabling them to exchange views on the subject with persons from entirely different socio-economic backgrounds.

b)   a careful selection of witnesses which is made so that the participants are informed in a balanced way about the relevant issues.

c)   the facilitators ensuring that the very different participants meet with mutual respect and ensure that citizens hear the contributions of all participants during the deliberations.[86]

Different models which use the "Mini Publics"

- Planning cells: Approx. 25 randomly selected citizens corresponding to a representative section of the population. In one to two weeks, they work in groups to propose solutions to a specific planning problem and are paid by the state. The aim is to prepare a citizen's opinion. To this end, at least four of these cells are applied to a very complex problem, some of which are even regarded as un-solvable. These can be combined with a group of the most important stakeholders of the different interests. These collectively determine the scope of the expert statements and the selection of the experts in advance.

- Citizen Assembly: 100 to 200 randomly selected citizens as a representative section of the population. Experts give them a balanced and intensive introduction to the topic. The group can then request further experts to listen to and question them in order to clarify contradictions, open questions, etc. The group can then ask for further experts to be interviewed. The meeting then evaluates the arguments, develops proposals for solutions to the problem, votes on the alternatives and compiles a generally understandable report with a recommendation.

- Deliberative Poll: Several hundred randomly selected citizens as a representative section of the population. At the start, these citizens

---

[86] Graham Smith, Democratic Innovations: Designing Institutions for Citizen Participation (Theories of Institutional Design), p. 174

answer a questionnaire. They are then informed about the topic in question and discuss (see above). Then they fill in the same questionnaire again. In this way, an attempt is made to find whether the participants' opinion has changed as a result of the intensive discussion of the topic. "Deliberative polls model what the public thinks, even if the public does not think much about the topic and has not dealt with the topic. Deliberative polls try to model what the public would think if they were given a better opportunity to think more intensely about the question."[87]

- Participatory Budgeting: Originally introduced in the Brazilian city of Porto Alegre in 1989, the Participatory Budgeting model gives citizens the opportunity to co-determine the use of part of the public budget. The model combines different forms of participation. General meetings at the neighborhood and regional level in Porto Alegre in 2001 led to the participation of a total of 16,600 citizens. In these meetings, citizens are elected to represent them in forums where decisions on the distribution of resources are taken. The regional budget forums are complemented by thematic ones. Members of all regional and thematic budget fora and direct repre-senttatives of the regional and thematic general assembly's form the Council of the Participatory Budget. Together with the mayor's office, this determines the predetermined fixed part of the budget.[88]

You could supplement the presence formats presented above with open discussions on an internet platform. Interested citizens could follow the progress of the assembly and discuss it, and if necessary, also interact with it.

---

[87] James S. Fishkin, The Voice of the People, p. 162
[88] Graham Smith, Democratic Innovations: Designing Institutions for Citizen Participation (Theories of Institutional Design), p. 34 ff

This can be achieved via an input mechanism or the participation in the mini publics in the discussion forum.

Examples for experiences with Mini Publics

One example is the Citizens' Assembly of the Canadian province of British Columbia. In 2004, it assembled a group of 160 randomly selected citizens to examine the electoral system and make proposals for its reform. They voted in favor of the STV (Single Transferable Vote) procedure used by Ireland, Australia, and Malta for their national elections. A majority of voters (57% in total), then adopted the recommendation. However, it was not implemented due to the 60% threshold previously set.

A second example is the Citizens' Initiative Review Process of the US state of Oregon. Before each referendum, a panel of 24 randomly selected citizens convenes for a few days. This group listens to both sides and consults scientific experts to gain in-depth knowledge and carefully analyzes the issue before issuing a public statement. This is written in everyday language and is a maximum of two or three pages long. It contains the core findings, a brief summary of the group members who are for and against the initiative, and other relevant key considerations. The number of votes for and against the initiative is clearly visible. The same applies to the individual arguments, so that voters can clearly see how convincing each was for the group participants. The full statement will be attached to the electoral brochure, which all voters will receive by letter. According to research by Professor John Gastil and his colleagues at Pennsylvania State University, the comments not only lead to an increase in voters' knowledge of the subject, but also have a significant impact on their voting behavior.[89]

The above-mentioned example of co-determined budgeting is Porto Alegre in Brazil. The previously prevalent corruption has been greatly reduced and replaced by a more open and transparent form of government. The structure has led to a significant increase in the active participation of poorer sections of the population - sections of the population that are traditionally very underrepresented in the political system. The process has led to a redistribution of prestige projects to infrastructure projects of daily use. This has systematically led to a preference in the budget distribution for poorer districts, which were previously often neglected by the administration. Since then, the model has been used in various other cities.[90]

Mini Publics - Attack Vectors

Of course, you have to be aware of the weaknesses of these mini publics, especially how they can potentially be influenced:

1.  The assignment to a Mini Public can be placed in such a way that critical topics are not considered at all or the question is already heading for a certain solution.

2.  The group can be given one-sided preliminary information in order to steer it in a certain direction.

3.  If a random selection can be manipulated, participants can be introduced into the group who try to steer in a certain direction.

---

[89] Manuel Arriagna, Rebooting Democracy: A Citizen's Guide to Reinventing Politics, p. 48 f

[90] Graham Smith, Democratic Innovations: Designing Institutions for Citizen Participation (Theories of Institutional Design), p. 34 ff and https://www.participatorybudgeting.org/pb-map

4. Invited lobbyists could try to intimidate the participants in a small circle.

5. The facilitators can steer the participants in one direction or away from another.

A preventive measure against points 1, 2, and 3 would be a nationally prescribed standard process for the drafting of mini publics. This ensures that all interest groups are informed. They can participate in the compilation of the group of stakeholders and experts etc. who will present their input. A potential countermeasure to point 4 would be a live broadcast of all hearings of stakeholders and experts. Countermeasures against point 5 can include rules of conduct for facilitators on the basis of which the participants can evaluate the moderators and if necessary, exclude biased moderators.

Studies on the results of the Mini Publics

The results of many studies give very good marks to the new participatory models. From a comprehensive empirical study on Citizen Deliberation by Prof. John Dryzek, Political Sciences, Australian National University:

> "The most obvious finding is that, given the opportunity, ordinary citizens can make good deliberators. Moreover, issue complexity is no barrier to the development and exercise of that competence." [91]

Results from two decades of citizen panels run by Prof. James Fishkin, Political Science and Communication, Stanford University:

"The public is very smart if you give it a chance. If people think their voice actually matters, they'll do the hard work, really study...ask the experts informed questions and then make tough decisions. When they hear experts disagreeing, they're forced to think for themselves. About 70% change their

---

[91] Manuel Arriagna, Rebooting Democracy: A Citizen's Guide to Reinventing Politics, p. 43

minds in the process. Citizens can become better informed and master the most complex issues of state government if they are given the chance."[92]

2010 after intensive research of two citizen panels, Prof. John Gastil, Communications, Penn State University and PhD student Katherine Knobloch:

> Participants engaged in "high-quality deliberation" characterized by a "rigorous analysis of the issues." These citizens "carefully analyzed the issues put before them and maintained a fair and respectful discussion throughout the proceedings." The statements produced by the two citizen panels at the end of the process "included almost all of the key insights and arguments that emerged during their meetings, and…were free of any gross factual errors or logical fallacies."[93]

It has been shown that "normal" people have the ability to draw up analyses and proposals for action oriented towards the common good, even when dealing with complicated political issues. They only have to be given enough time and their debate must not be one-sidedly restricted or distorted by economic or political interest groups. These positive experiences point to the success potential for the Proxy Party's work, which is similar in process.


Higher representation legitimation of Mini Publics

In contrast to politicians, most of whom come only from the middle or upper class, a representative group selected by chance has greater legitimacy to represent the entire population. The group is given sufficient time and resources to inform itself on a topic from all sides and to make a well-

---

92 Manuel Arriagna, p. 43
93 Manuel Arriagna, p. 43-44

considered and balanced judgement. They are thus far better off than the average voter (and also the average elected representative). The average voter has enough to do with his own life to be able to inform himself in detail about all topics. He usually limits himself to a few secondary sources, which according to confirmation bias, reinforce his existing opinion. Since he does not have the time, he often decides based on a gut feeling. And this can be easily manipulated by interest groups. Well-funded groups have far better chances to package their message professionally and deliver it effectively optimized or even individualized.

An article by the Guardian analyses the rather chaotic way to Brexit. It discusses the alternatives to democratic voting processes, advocates the wider use of mini publics, and lists the following advantages:

> "Sortition could provide a remedy to the democratic fatigue syndrome that we see everywhere today. The drawing of lots is not a miracle cure any more than elections ever were, but it can help correct a number of the faults in the current system. The risk of corruption is reduced, election fever abates and attention to the common good increases. Voting on the basis of gut feeling is replaced by sensible deliberation, as those who have been drafted are exposed to expert opinion, objective information and public debate. Citizens chosen by lot may not have the expertise of professional politicians, but they add something vital to the process: freedom. After all, they don't need to be elected or re-elected."[94]

---

[94] https://www.theguardian.com/politics/2016/jun/29/why-elections-are-bad-for-democracy

## 8.4 (Is there a) Danger of oppression of minorities?

> "Democracy is the worst of all forms of government – apart from all the other forms that have been tried from time to time."
> -Winston Churchill

The main challenge is that the majority determines the life of the minority:

> "If you think about it, you must come to the conclusion that the basic mechanism of democracy - the fact that the majority is in the lead - is essentially immoral, and in a democracy moral consideration is trumped by the will of the majority. Quantity trumps quality - the number of people who want something overrides considerations of morality and rationality."[95]
> -Karel Beckman, Author and Journalist

This concern is valid. However, if you compare pure parliamentary democracy and one that is complemented with elements of direct democracy, you may find that direct democracy performs better in this regard. Both have the described problem. In parliamentary democracy however, there is the additional problem that the minority can also rule the majority in individual questions. The result may be wrong qualitatively and quantitatively as well as morally and rationally. A good example of this, is currently found in US politics: well over 80% of voters are in favor of net neutrality, but maintaining it seems not achievable.[96]

> Another author gives us a hint in his warning:
> "Unrestricted democracy is, just like oligarchy, a tyranny extended

---

[95] Translated from: Karel Beckmann, Wenn die Demokratie zusammenbricht: Warum uns das demokratische Prinzip in eine Sackgasse führt, p. 39
[96] https://medium.com/s/story/its-time-to-stop-ignoring-tech-policy-at-the-ballot-box-95f576359fba

to a large group of people."

-Aristotle

Following the logic of this great thinker, there are three ways of avoiding tyranny:

- Setting absolute limits for the rights of intervention of the state, such as through the establishment of inalienable fundamental rights
- Restricting the sphere of influence of the state so that the state can intervene in the lives of people only in the absolutely necessary areas
- Defining rules for writing laws that make it difficult to favor or discriminate against groups

Absolute limits to the rights of intervention of the state

The first requirement is largely implemented, e.g. in the Universal Declaration of Human Rights of the UN General Assembly. At the federal level, these rights can be found in Articles 1 to 13 of the German Grundgesetz (preliminary constitution, 70years old) and in the US Constitution and its Amendments.


**Limitation of the sphere of influence of the state**

The second arrangement, not to make the majority a dictator of minorities, is to make the state "minimally invasive." The state should give every citizen a chance to live a self-determined life. This should be achieved with the least possible administrative burden.

Only when other people are affected in their freedom should the state set up rules for these interactions between the interacting parties. If these rules are violated, the state must ensure that a fair arbitration is reached and enforced.

This raises the question of the scope of the state and the optimum between the two poles: "Leave us alone!" and "Take care of us all!"

It must be remembered that the state unfortunately tends to grow:

- The average politician likes to make and keep promises, which means he needs more redistribution power.
- An administrative apparatus tends to expand.
- The requests from different stakeholders for compensation or special treatment are increasing rather than decreasing.

Only the limited budget ensures an upper limit. Even this is not absolute. In general, politicians like to borrow. Today's voters calling for benefits are more important to them than the deteriorating situation they create in the future, e.g. the continued destruction of the environment.

A combination of the desire: "Leave us alone!" and "Take care of us all!" could look like this:

a)  Reduce the redistribution volume to the necessary

b)  Restrict the possibilities of extending the redistribution volume by law

c)  Introduce an unconditional basic income, which covers the basic needs of the people and the "Take care of us all!" aspect.

The result would be a more humane social system than today. Very few would receive additional benefits due to individual hardship. The new system would require only a fraction of today's administrative burden. It would take away fundamental challenges and allow for the people's free development.

## Avoid favoring or discriminating against groups

It would be optimal if there were no laws that give a particular group an advantage or disadvantaged a group. It should be remembered that many of today's anti-discrimination measures are not mere protection, but in fact, prefer a group. Exceptions to this principle should be considered with utmost care.

Benefits should not be given to individuals or groups, but only actions that support the achievement of defined goals. Thus, a good legal and tax system could consistently support the achievement of socially agreed goals.

Example objective: "Reduction of the ecological footprint of the country and its inhabitants:"

- Reduced tax rate for all products and services that directly transition to a sustainable energy supply
- Increased tax rate for private cars, meat, marine diesel, cruise ships, etc.

If such a maxim of non-favoring could be established and if the main supportable goals are limited to a maximum of two or three, it would be much easier to keep the proliferation of clientele-driven laws in check. Exceptions could only be accepted with a 2/3 majority or in a public referendum and would be broadly discussed in the media to form a consensus.

## 8.5 Some important policy decisions

Many important topics stand little chance to be discussed in our parliaments in the foreseeable future. In many cases, this is a result of the fact that the political and public apparatus hardly questions itself. After all, it lives quite comfortably in its self-created mostly non-efficiency driven, and responsibility free environment.

As argued in Chapters 13 and 14, the proxy party should base itself on the topics "democracy" and "transparency". But, it needs to develop its own voice on other topics to be successful in elections.

You can find a list of other important political topics in Appendix IV. I recommend reading and I promise you will find a lot of interesting ideas.

## Summary

The fears of critics that an agitated crowd makes the wrong decision is generally justified. This danger can however, be mitigated to a large extent by time constraints. This gives the citizen sufficient time to inform himself about the issue. Limitations on state power and freedom of choice, as well as a consideration of the fundamental rights of individuals, can further contribute to ensuring that no laws or measures are passed that favor or disadvantage individual groups.

A US survey largely refutes the assumption that the people can be influenced by interest groups.

In principle, important decisions belong in the hands of those affected, i.e. the population. This is not the case in Germany, even with the most important decisions. As a result, many important issues are not pursued or do not even reach parliament.

New, already positively tested political instruments of representation, such as mini publics or planning cells, are available to shift some of the decisions back to the citizen.

83

# Part II

# SOLUTION APPROACH

# 9. Not a new party, but a new breed of party

As explained in the previous chapters, the party-controlled parliamentary democracy has many disadvantages:

A.    Problems of voters with politicians and their policies

- Many voters do not believe that the politicians represent them. A study on this subject agrees and speaks of a "crisis of representation."

- Too often, politicians decide in favor of a resolution even if a majority of the population is opposed to it.

- The confidence of the population in politicians is very low.

- People's disenchantment with politics is increasing, as they cannot change anything, no matter who they vote for.

B. Democratic problems of the parties and parliamentary work

- Almost all established parties are not democratically organized internally. Votes of the party base are rare. In some cases, decisions are enforced by the party leadership against the majority of the party base.

- Decision making in a parliamentary democracy is essentially based on small groups of people making or preparing decisions. These are far easier to influence than larger groups.

C. Problems of democratic institutions and self-service

- The three pillars of democracy are not correctly set up in Germany. The judiciary is controlled in decisive points by the executive, in this case, the Ministry of Justice.

- The parties and the representatives have too much influence on other institutions, even those they are controlled by, especially through the right of appointment.

- The measures to prevent representatives from being influenced are often inadequate (anti-bribery laws).

- The established parties are very heavily financed by the state.

A complex bundle of problems.

And the established parties have no interest in unravelling and solving them.

The problems mentioned under C. can only be tackled on a long-term basis. The problems mentioned under A. and B. can be tackled in the medium term. It is particularly important that a credible alternative is offered.

"You will never change things by fighting the existing.

To change something, build a new model

that makes the old one superfluous."

- Buckminster Fuller, renowned 20th century inventor and visionary

But where will the trust for a new party come from?

In the end, it's all the same, but in a different flavor: Every four years, we have an election and then the political parties do what they want, again. Even those that start as a "big alternative" are absorbed by the party system over time.

Trust in parties has been eroded by the established parties.

## 9.1 Trust alone, is not enough

But what can be done if the voters no longer trust the promises of the parties and even new parties are under general suspicion? How can a new party differ noticeably from the old parties? How can a party reach the disillusioned and credibly assure that things will be different this time?

In my opinion, the answer is not "just set up a party and an election program." Both, after all, are again just…promises.

The voter needs more than just promises to restore his confidence in political parties. He needs assurances:

- Assurances that the party leadership will not detach from the party base and voters
- Assurances that the party base is not only allowed to discuss topics, but can also have a say in the decision itself
- Assurance that the topic preparation is neutral and solution-oriented

- Assurance that the decisions reached by the party will be comprehensible

- Assurances that the influence of lobbyists will be balanced with that of scientists, NGOs, and citizens' initiatives, etc.

- Built-in control mechanisms that the procedures are adhered to.

## 9.2 Prove trustworthiness

If we are serious about strengthening democracy, we must rethink the party as a vehicle for representing democratic interests. We cannot continue to rely solely on the conscience of representatives and the self-regulation of the actors.

The system of a new party and its processes must be trustworthy and must ensure that the rules of democracy are respected. It must still produce good results even if several participants deliberately try to undermine it. This also applies, or even in particular, if the party leadership attempts to do so.

In order to find solutions for the reorganization of a new type of party, we can take inspiration from the blockchain technology.

A blockchain is trustworthy because an incorruptible third-party records everything and you can refer to it. It is practically impossible to cheat or so costly that the effort doesn't match the yield. The strength of the system lies in its decentralization. This incorruptible third party is not a single person who can be bribed or forced to falsify data. Instead, the blockchain creates a decentralized consensus about the truth across all participants. It comes to the correct result even if up to 49% of the participants try to cheat.

Unfortunately, the principle cannot be applied 1:1 to politics because "THE Truth" does not exist.

But what can be transferred from this idea and looked at are:

a)  Equal vote rating in the decision, including the representative weighted vote in parliament (grassroots democracy with 1:1 representation)

b)  Inner-party processes, such as the execution of inner-party votes (adherence to process steps)

c)  Maintaining the integrity of the evidence of the execution of the processes and of the results (no changes to them)

These steps alone would very clearly make the processes of the new party far more democratic and transparent than those of all established parties.

As described, results can be influenced by the targeted selection of the underlying information. By omitting facts, framing terms, the use of half-truths and other manipulations, the basis for voting can easily steer the results.

In order to ensure the democratic execution of coordination processes based on topic inputs, it is essential to review these inputs as well:

- correctness of the provided basis data incl. source checking
- completeness of the most important facts and arguments (90:10 approach)
- neutrality of the comparison of the arguments

To make the thematic votes of the party demonstrably democratic, the inputs as well as the results must be published.

Audited content input

+ Checked compliance with the processes

+ Non-modifiable publication of test contents and results

= Verifiable safeguarding of democratic processes

The "internal degree of democracy" of parties would be comparable. However, external independent experts would be required for a trustworthy audit. In fact, a central independent preparation of the underlying facts, cause-and-effect relationships, etc., would be more efficient. This could then be used as an input by all parties. Only the recommendation for each party basis would be different, since it is based on the values and belief system of the respective party.

Even if it is possible to create the perfect basis for decision-making, many party members will not be sufficiently concerned with it. They will make their decision primarily on the basis of their preconceived opinions. And, as described in Chapter 7.5, this will be shaped primarily by the media. In this respect, a party that advocates democratic voting must also deal with the subject of the media.

## Summary

Through their actions, the established parties have lost the trust of citizens. In order to regain the confidence of voters, this new party should not simply work with promises as did the old parties. Instead, the party should offer assurances that it weighs topics and their solutions rationally, is democratically organized within the party, and actually represents voters in their interests. To be credible, these safeguards should be verifiable.

To ensure a democratic process, both the input and the processes need to be examined. The audit results must be immutable and made available at least to the party members.

# 10. Proxy Party as Way to Direct Democracy

As discussed in the previous chapters, the incumbent parties are the cause of many problems. This does not necessarily apply to the individual representatives of these parties, but to the whole construct. The structural difficulties discussed in the book and the studies mentioned, raise strong doubts that the incumbent parties represent their constituents.

If we want to achieve better voter representation, we need to rethink. If we go down the existing path again and just "hope" for the best, we shouldn't wonder if the results don't improve.

How about, for a change, if we elected a party ...

> ... in which you can not only discuss, but also have a say?
>
> ... in which elected representatives commit themselves to vote 1:1 as the party base decides?
>
> ... which focuses on strengthening direct democracy and political transparency?
>
> .. which concentrates on common ground in order to advance important issues?

... which tries to get to the bottom of the difficulties and doesn't restrict itself to politically correct thoughts to keep the full spectrum for analysis and solutions of problems

... that lives direct democracy and provides its members with well-prepared, neutral decision-making alternatives and informs them about the expected consequences of the alternatives?

... which demonstrably safeguards and makes transparent the democratic processes within the party, while at the same time working efficiently?

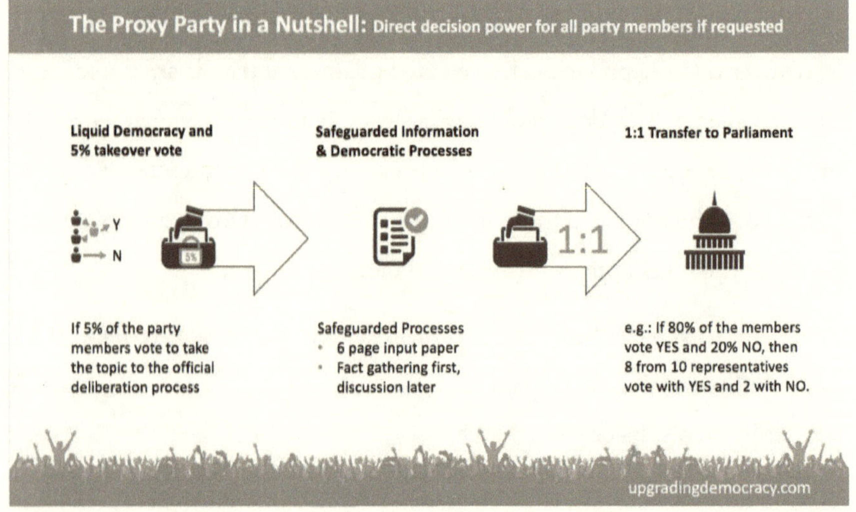


I you are interested you can find a shareable version of this graphic on my website upgradingdemocracy.com.

## 10.1 Why a Proxy Party?

Today's political parties show considerable democratic deficits. The individual party members have a minimal say outside of the election of their leaders. The transparency of the decisions taken is often vague. The party leadership sets official topics and thus restricts the field of discussion.

The regular members of the parties are not involved in the process of establishing the basis for decision-making. This process usually takes place in back rooms. This offers many opportunities for internal and external influence.

During the actual "exercise of power," i.e. the vote in Parliament, the regular members of the party have no means of getting their way. In fact, votes are taken as decided by the party leadership. Dissenting opinions are not relevant. In extreme cases, the representatives of a party even vote against the will of the majority of its members.

This undemocratic approach does not ensure a fair representation of party members. The result is an increasing alienation of the members from their party. At the same time, the parties have alienated themselves from their constituents, who feel that they can only vote for "the lesser evil." In countries like the US and the UK, where the party with the most votes win, citizens are stuck with two bad choices.

The alternative would be a party that takes grassroots democracy seriously. The most important steps in the process must be safeguarded by democratic mechanisms and controls:

- a) Identification of topics
- b) Election of representatives of the party
- c) Filling of list positions
- d) Preparation of the basis for decisions

e) Parliamentary votes

However, this grassroots democratic approach must be implemented very efficiently. Otherwise this might lead to never-ending discussions. More on this in the following chapters.

## 10.2 Proxy Party and proxy representative

> "In computer networks, a proxy server is a server (computer) which clients (people or computers) use to access other computers…A proxy server that passes information to its clients without changing it is usually called a gateway or sometimes tunneling proxy."[97]

A Proxy Party is a party that acts as a mediator between party members and political decision-makers. It facilitates the formation of opinion. All party members vote on the subject. The representatives of the Proxy Party then vote in exactly the same way as the party members' voting weights have determined in advance.

A Proxy Representative is a party member of a party described above. He pledges to vote with his fellow members in exactly the same way as the voting weights of the party members have determined in advance. For example: After a discussion with all party members, 70% of them vote "yes," 20% for "no," and 10% abstain. In the appropriate vote, 7 of 10 representatives will vote "yes," 2 with "no," and one abstains.

---

[97] https://en.wikipedia.org/wiki/Proxy_server

## 10.3 Proxy Party as a Way to Direct Democracy

If you take this principle further and 100% of the voters voted for this party, a direct democracy would become a reality. This would be limited however, since de facto, only the party members would have a say, but not the entire electorate.

As soon as the Proxy Party achieves greater significance, it will strengthen and expand direct-democratic elements. It will strive for the introduction of a nationwide referendum. It will discuss whether referendums should be supplemented by mandatory planning cells (see Chapter 8.3) that would create a recommendation. These would have to be set up and implemented according to predefined criteria. The compliance of the processes would have to be monitored. It should be considered whether a third proposal variant for nationwide referendums (compromise proposal) has to be introduced to the vote if this is desired by one side.

Alternatives to the current type of democracy should be discussed with the aim to strengthen the representation of all classes. An example would be a representative parliament by lot, as outlined in the book *The End of Politicians* by Brett Hennig. Another example would be a representative assembly of citizens selected by lot. This assembly periodically examines the leadership of the state and structurally improves it, as presented in the book *Rebooting Democracy*. It focuses on setting the right rules and incentives so that elected politicians represent public interest.

## 10.4 Liquid Democracy in the Proxy Party

The concept of "liquid democracy" has several different characteristics. Basically, every concept wants to supplement or even replace parliamentary democracy with a direct democracy. This allows the flexible, short-term, and thematic transfer of votes ("delegated voting") to a person to be believed to have expertise on a subject or a similar attitude to one's own. Votes can also be delegated to a group. In this case the delegated vote accepts the majority opinion of the group members.

In order to enable the procedure described above even with large numbers of voters, the processes are supported and secured by IT systems.

## 10.5 What are the roles of elected representatives?

Representatives must see themselves as "direct proxies" of party members. They should therefore have no problem voting as these have determined. Apart from that, they also have other tasks to perform:

1) Be present in the plenary hall and use their votes to represent the party members
2) Explore issues with other political parties and find allies to advance the party's proposals
3) Suggest actions that advance the core issues of the party
4) Give input for the thematic decision papers
5) Use speaking time to demand more transparency and democracy in political work and to advance other neglected issues
6) Promote the idea of the party to the press.

## 10.6 Must there be a party leadership? What tasks does it have?

To be successful, the party must successfully communicate its grassroots approach, values, and actions. This requires credible, convincing, and rhetorically well-trained people.

Since the press wants to have central contact persons and usually talks to the party leadership, these two functions should be combined. The party law of your country might even demand that party leaders must be appointed. However, the party leadership should consist of two or even three people to illustrate the grassroots democratic idea behind the party. With this approach, the party only needs two to three PR professionals. But of course, other members can also be active, in their respective field of expertise.

## Summary

The Proxy Party is a grassroots democratic alternative to the classical party. The party member has a say even after the election of the party chairman and can exercise this directly or indirectly in each vote. The representatives are the transmitters of the will of all party members.

The Proxy Party is focused on making its decisions and the choice of topics as democratic and transparent as possible. It will try to extend these principles to the entire political system.

# 11. Appointment of candidates

In a typical voting system, the constituents can either vote for direct candidates or for party lists with candidates. In the latter case the candidates on the lists and their position on the list are determined by the party. The number of votes reached, determines the composition of the seats in parliament by the parties. Members are appointed in the order in which they are listed.

The following decisions must therefore be taken within the party before the candidates are determined:

a)   who will run as a direct candidate for the new party in the respective constituency?

b)   which candidates will be added to the party list?

c)   the order in which the party's candidates are included on the party's list.

## 11.1 Profile of Direct Election Candidates

The following qualifications are important for direct candidates:

Primary qualification: The candidate should be able to win the direct election.

Secondary qualifications: To be elected and later to be a good representative:

a)  Internalization of the task as representative of his voters, including the inconvenient direct democratic basic orientation.

b)  Persuasiveness

- Can express him/herself well and explain complex topics to different groups

- Is politically broadly educated

- Is open and honest

- Is authentic.

c)  Is fact-oriented and wants to advance topics. Is in a position to focus on commonalities and to advance topics on the basis of these.

d)  Is not an egomaniac.

e)  Is not a dogmatist. Is able to question himself and his positions and to look at both sides objectively. Can accept when others decide differently because of a different weighting of arguments or a different value background.

f)  Good in comprehensible thematic preparation and mediation of topics.

g)  Expert in one or more socially relevant subject areas.

h)  Wants to change society for the better and is solution-oriented and efficient in doing so.

The profile for direct candidates is certainly not complete. But the above list should provide a good starting point for discussion.

## 11.2 Profile of List Candidates

Since the list candidates do not have to be directly elected, the aspects of a "gifted seller of the idea" mentioned in 11.1 are not that important. The secondary qualifications mentioned are more relevant, in particular, the ability to structure, prepare, and communicate topics.

The aim should be to have independent topic experts elected to parliament via the list election. In this way, possible committee and committee positions can be assigned to specialists. These specialists can make a critical contribution and facilitate the internal formation of opinion within the party, e.g. in internal working groups.

It would also be helpful if some PR-experienced professionals could be recruited and elected. They should be well versed in working with the media, especially with very critical media. Marketing specialists, especially those with knowledge of social media campaigns, are also very important. At a later date, many of these tasks can be taken over by employees of the party. In the early stages of the party however, this will not necessarily be the case.

It would also be very helpful if some listed candidates had experience as moderators. There are many topics to discuss. A professional facilitation would make opinion forming more efficient and trouble-free.

## 11.3 Appointment of candidates on the basis of a better voting system

Election of candidates

The candidates for the constituency shall be determined by the party members of the constituency concerned. The same applies synonymously at the level of the federal states and at the national level.

Every party member can (if he or she is eligible for election in accordance with the respective laws) run for an office or for the selection of direct candidates or for list seats.

Each candidate has the opportunity to present himself in a fixed format on the party website and to actively participate in internal party discussions. In addition, he is free to refer to more detailed websites on his profile.

Party internal electoral system

Very often, an electoral system is used to determine candidates, which provides for an election in two rounds:

> 1st Round: Each eligible voter votes for one candidate. Determination: If none of the candidates achieves a 50% majority, a run-off vote is held between the two candidates with the most votes from the first round.
>
> 2nd Round: In the run-off, the candidate with the most votes wins.

This electoral system leads to a political choice in the 1st round, as the voter has to consider who of the candidates has a chance to make it into the run-off election. Otherwise it can easily happen that he "wastes" his own vote on a candidate who has no chance. This might even lead to the second-best candidate being weakened and not being elected to the second ballot.

Other systems reflect the preferences of the voters much better:

> Borda vote: The count is based on the voter's candidate rankings. The first place gets the most points, the second place gets one point less, and the third place gets one point less than that, and so on. Often, only three points, two points, and one point are awarded for the first three candidates. The candidate with the highest total score wins. The only difficulty is to make the voting documents so clear

that it is clear whether the voter is awarding 3 points or marking the third place.

Bucklin's vote: The count is based on the voter's candidate rankings. However, the system checks whether one of the candidates has an absolute majority of the initial preferences, then this candidate is elected. Otherwise, the second preferences of all voters are added to the first preferences. This is continued until either one of the candidates has an absolute majority or all placings are counted and the candidate with the most votes is determined as the winner.

There are also other procedures that allow those candidates to be eliminated who were most often elected to last place (Coombs vote) or those who received the least initial preferences (Instant Runoff vote).

The Janecek Method[98] which gives each voter the option to give each candidate a YES or NO vote is also quite promising. You might also use a value between -1 and +1 to enable a very nuanced vote.

The selection of the appropriate voting right is relevant. The only important thing, however, is that the will of the voters is not influenced by tactical considerations. The voting result should optimally reflect the will of the voters.


Open elections

If the election takes place openly, dissenters may be subject to repression by the current party leadership, especially if it "nevertheless wins again." Therefore, an open election of candidates is not a good choice.

---

[98] https://www.ih21.org/en/janecek-method

## Summary

The profile of a direct election candidate of the Proxy Party is on the one hand, very similar to that of a candidate of other parties. He has to be able to "sell" the idea of the party and has to have the necessary skills. On the other hand, he must be able to withdraw in order to fit into the grassroots democratic structures in his later work. Egomaniacs are not welcome.

Ideal candidates have expert knowledge in at least one socially relevant topic and can discuss and communicate this in an understandable way. They want to change society for the better and are solution-oriented and efficient. They have a very healthy understanding of real democracy and tolerance for other points of view. They are able to lead to common ground and drive forward changes on this basis.

The ability to structure, prepare, and communicate topics is more important for the list candidate. Topic experts and candidates with PR, social media, and moderation experience should be preferred.

The electoral system has to enable the voters to express their will uninfluenced by electoral tactical considerations. It has to optimally reflect the will of the voters. This demands a different than normal voting system.

# 12. Finding topics and voting on them

The Proxy Party focuses on efficiently safeguarding intra-party democratic processes and implementing the results developed in the processes.

Important points of the content-related work are above all to:

- efficiently pick up new topics

- efficiently weight the incoming topics with the members

- efficiently prepare important topics

- efficiently generate opinion

- determine if the topic should be included in the Priority Program

- restrict reopening of topics already discussed in order to be able to advance thematically (prerequisite for a re-introduction, i.e.: if decisive facts have changed and the majority is in favor of a reopening or if a 2/3 majority opts to reopen the topic).

This version 1.0 of the sketch for a potential organization of the topic identification and topic coordination, surely still has to be completed:

1. Input of topics by individual members on the basis of a 2-page-template form "Why is the topic important?" including a half-page abstract. These must receive a minimum number of votes (e.g. 60%) in a member preliminary

vote of less than 1% randomly selected members (but at least 50 members). If a member does not respond within a certain period of time, he will be replaced by an alternate member. Instead of a simple yes/no alternative, another point system is used. Example: Five rating options "completely unimportant" (0%) / "not important" (25%) / "neutral" (50%) / "important" (75%) / "very important" (100%).

A good preparation of the topic is very important. If the topic is well described and logically structured, many members will decide in favor of dealing with it and will proceed in the process. In order to reduce the expected flood of topics and increase their quality, a topic is not allowed to be submitted for voting without an initial preparation. If a member should not be able to prepare the topic, he can search for and win other members for the preparation on the platform of the party.

In the first few months, it is advisable to concentrate on two core themes of the party: "democracy" and "transparency" (see Chapter 14). This can quickly create a well-coordinated and coherent basis on which the party can build for other topics.

2. The priorities for processing are determined by the approval rate of the topics. If a topic has 86% approval, then this is prioritized over a topic which reached only 82%. This, however, is relativized by the support of the party members. If only a few members are active and if no qualified topic preparation is achieved, the topic is postponed.

3. Structured discussion of the topic, on the basis of standardized thematic decision templates. All papers should contain in-depth links. Factual claims such as numbers must include a reference to a trustworthy source. Whenever possible a link to the base data must be included. All participants taking part in the creation of the document must disclose in which way and how strongly

they could be biased. All users that are able to change the document itself have to register and proof their expertise in the respective areas.

The topic experts among party members are responsible for quality assurance. Everyone must be aware that a 6-page presentation of a topic cannot fully reflect it. But even an 80% or 90% solution is far better than anything that today's policy achieves.

> 2-page introduction and facts
>
> 1-page sketch effect relationships
>
> 1-Page pro-argumentation
>
> 1-page counter-argumentation incl. risks
>
> 1-page recommendation of the board of directors or the circle of experts on the basis of the party's fundamental values

The interdependencies are shown in a graphical representation which includes the most important factors and results. This illustrates how individual factors influence the outcome.

4. During the actual discussion in the forums with in-depth links, objective and solution-oriented discussions are held. Personal attacks and other disturbing actions lead to temporary or permanent exclusion from the discussion. Relevant attacks are to be defined even more precisely as rules of the game. Above all, the rules have to focus on efficiency. Otherwise, this part of the thematic coordination will quickly degenerate into a lot of work and can lead to a standstill. This also includes the fact that the number of words (online discussion) or time (face-to-face discussion) per discussion participant is limited. They are only allowed to write more if other participants mark the previous contributions as valuable.

5. Potential adaptation of the draft sketched under Point 3, based on the outcomes of the discussion.

6. Not all members will have interest or time to discuss or vote on all topics. Therefore, a "topic-based delegate system" based on blockchain technology will be established (Liquid Democracy). Here, each party member can delegate his vote completely or for topic areas to another member. 24 hours before the election date, the election system sends the information on how the delegate vote is used, to the member. A notification with a request to log-in or an encrypted dispatch is used. The voting delegation can be cancelled by the member at any time. The vote on a topic can be overwritten with a personally cast vote at any time.

7. Determination of the voting share of the party members and transfer to the deputies, e.g. 70% YES / 20% NO / 10% abstention = with 10 deputies seven vote for YES, two for NO, and one abstains.

Distribution of votes according to the preference of representatives.

It should be achieved that as many deputies as possible can vote as they would vote on their own initiative. The obligation to vote differently in order to represent the voting weight of the party members as 1:1 as possible, is minimized by the vote distribution system. The coercion is evenly distributed so that this democratic burden is evenly distributed.

8. It is recorded how the individual representatives of that party voted and reconciled with the system's inputs. The representatives should have voted in exactly the same way as was pre-determined by the weighting of party members and the allocation of the vote distribution system. In the case of roll-call votes, this is officially recorded. In the case of anonymous parliamentary votes, a way is found in uncovering differences. The party will work to ensure, that in principle, all thematic parliamentary votes are taken by name.

9. Transparent publication on the party's website:

- Party internal thematical decision papers based on templates (published before the vote)

- How each representative will vote (published before the vote)

- Comparison of the voting behavior of the party members (recorded via the blockchain) with the voting behavior of the representatives. Consistency in %.

- All documents are secured by a blockchain (time stamp).

- There is no external commentary function for the decision-papers in order not to slow down the party's work. 100% perfection can never be achieved on complex issues.

The published thematical decision papers may also be consulted by party members of other parties. This may put parties with a more centralist organization under "democratic pressure."

Of course, voting in the Proxy Party could also be also conducted more traditionally. As with other parties, voting would then be as uniform as a bloc. The important difference to the normal party: The instruction for the vote would not come from the party leadership, but from the party base. This traditional procedure, however, would not pass on the votes of the party base unfiltered and thus no longer reflect the will of the base 1:1.

Thoughts on determining the party's core topics can be found in Chapters 12 and 13.


## Summary

The inclusion of topics is subject to a grassroots democratic process. Just as with a referendum, the subject must reach certain thresholds before it is dealt with by other party members. The order of topics is determined by the voting results and the thematic capacities.

The topic input is structured, and discussions are fact-oriented, constructive and solution-oriented. This is the basis for an efficient analysis and consultation on the inclusion of new topics in the Party's work. The vote itself takes place in individually or via subject delegates (Liquid Democracy). Members of the party vote as determined by the votes of the party base. A system ensures that there is as little deviation as possible between the personal opinion of the delegate and his voting behavior. In accordance with the principle of transparency the thematic decision, basis paper for the delegates votes and its results are published on the party's website.

# 13. Core topics of the Proxy Party

What should be the topics of the Proxy Party and why? What should constitute the thematic core of the party?

Grassroots democracy and its values are the core of the party. To achieve and maintain these, transparency is indispensable. Both together form the thematic cornerstones of the party. The party exemplifies these values and is committed to achieving both goals in politics.

The extended topic of "media" results from the two topics of grassroots democracy and transparency. I take it up so prominently in this book above all, because it is decisive for the formation of political opinion. Without the addition of transparency, the media can be abused to the detriment of democracy.

Other topics are probably not necessary for the party's core program. This deliberate thematic restriction ensures that the party:

a)   has a clear focus

b)   can position itself credibly and is clearly legitimated on many issues

This thematic restriction prevents the party from deterring potential members in the initial phase by prematurely selecting topics.

Further topics should be included in an extended party program. The split into a core program and an extended party program signals openness to new topics and the reassessment of existing topics. This makes the party more future proof than other parties.

## 13.1 Grassroots democracy

Many of the rules and processes of today's politics are not perceived as democratic. It is time to democratize politics itself.

The goal is a grassroots democratic policy that is transparent in its processes and actions. It must objectively analyze the results achieved by politics, judge them and use insights for improvement. Citizens have to know that the processes that safeguard democracy are being adhered to.

**Basic Democratic Transformation of Politics**

- Transformation of the political system. Adding strong direct-democratic elements to the representative system. Creation of a system that has a high "built-in" resistance to undemocratic influences.

- Nationwide referendums and popular initiatives at regional, state, and federal level with standardized, uniform, reasonable hurdles based on the Swiss model. The association "Mehr Demokratie e.V."[99] demands: Multi-stage process over a year or even several years, so that an "overboiling soul of the people" cannot spontaneously throw over everything established.

  Step 1: Collect 100,000 signatures

  Step 2: A referendum can be started within 18 months. The Federal Constitutional Court monitors the legality of the petition. If at least

---

[99] https://www.mehr-demokratie.de/

one million signatures are collected within nine months, a referendum can take place.

Step 3: Referendum with an alternative proposal drawn up by the Bundestag.

Additions to the model of "Mehr Demokratie e.V.":

- Additionally, a fact check of the contents by an independent authority should be installed and unproven facts are to be removed from the texts.

- Rules of the game for the support of petitions for referendums and decisions: Transparency. Who stands behind them? Who supports them and with how much money? Determination of a maximum budget. For petitions for a referendum and referendums, factually correct names and headlines must be chosen. The voter should not be deceived about the subject of the vote. It must be clear what a voter votes for when he votes. Equal times for the presentation of positions in public broadcast stations for each side.

- For each referendum and each popular initiative, three to five planning cells of 25 randomly drawn representative citizens should give a brief introduction to the subject and an assessment of the proposals in a way that can be understood by the general public and show their internal majority ratios in all details (see Chapter 8.3). In the case of petitions for a referendum, it may even be necessary to create an additional proposal. This helps to avoid a pure yes/no situation and possibly opens up a feasible middle ground.

- Discussion of a citizens' assembly at federal level, which is composed of randomly drawn representatives of the people. The representatives would be elected for four to five years and could not be re-elected. This third chamber can, with a two-thirds majority, stop the resolutions of the other chambers or demand changes. A blockade is dissolved by a referendum.[100]

- Direct election of the heads of the Federal and State Courts of Audit by the voters with pre-qualification by a group of experts.

- Direct election of the heads of the public broadcasters by the voters with pre-qualification by a group of experts.

## Increased democratization of Parliament

- Allocation of speaking rights and speaking time by the members and not by the chairmen of the political groups or the Bureau.

- Ban of the "whip" that enforces voting for the representatives in accordance with the will of their parties

- No vote without a minimum of representatives present. Very narrow definition of exceptions and explicit approval by the chairman of the assembly required.

- Ban of ad-hoc votes. Very narrow definition of exceptions for an accelerated voting procedure. Safeguard the democratic control weights, and explicit approval by the Chairman of the Assembly required.

- Roll-call votes in Parliament for thematic votes as default

---

[100] Manuel Arriagna, Rebooting Democracy: A Citizen's Guide to Reinventing Politics, p.51f

- Exclusive use of members of parliament's staff for parliamentary work instead of party work. Clear instruction of the parliament to the employees paid by it and effective control.

## Party and parliamentary funding

- Laws on the financing of political parties or representatives (decisions on their own behalf) will not come into force until the next legislative period.

- Change to a party financing system that no longer overfinances the large established parties and thus consolidates the status quo. Switch to a system in which the citizen can transfer his vouchers to a party eligible to vote for (democracy dollars). This already has been established in Seattle.[101]

- Party donations from companies are prohibited. Party donations from private individuals are permitted up to a maximum of 5,000 euros per year. Other corporate donations to political parties, such as stand fees at party conferences or advertisements in member magazines, are also prohibited.

## Electoral System

- Change to a ranking choice voting system (Coombs election). The last candidate or party is eliminated from the list. The votes of the voters who elected this party as the number one party shall be redistributed among the candidate(s)/party(s) to whom the respective voter has ranked 2nd. This makes tactical voting unnecessary and achieves a far better translation of the will of the

---

[101] https://www.seattle.gov/democracyvoucher/about-the-program

voters to elected parties/representatives. It will be easier for new political parties to pass the 5% hurdle. See Chapter 11.3 and a good explainer video[102] for a potential new US system. This system already has been achieved in Maine thanks to a group of very dedicated citizens.[103]

- Switch of digital voting systems to blockchain technology, which ensures that votes cannot be changed once they have been stored. This is achieved by hashing the transaction and linking them together in blocks. This "hashing" corresponds to a cryptographic seal and makes changes impossible. It transforms the original data into an alphanumeric code that changes very noticeably with the smallest changes to the original.

- Nationwide election of representatives instead of an election of regional representatives or 50:50 division between the two types to get fewer generalists and more experts elected to parliament.

- Introduction of an option on the ballot paper "none of the parties on the ballot paper are eligible for me to vote" or an alternative for "no candidates." This information makes it possible to distinguish between the groups of voters who do not like any of the choices provided and those who are not interested in politics.

- Dependence of the filling of parliamentary seats on voter turnout. For example, if only 75% vote, only 100% - (25%/2) = 87.5% of the seats are filled.

---

[102] https://www.youtube.com/watch?v=q6pC5IJirrY
[103] https://equalcitizens.us/kyle-bailey-on-bringing-ranked-choice-voting-to-maine/

## European Union

- Conversion of the EU from an elite project to a citizens' Europe of the regions

- Conversion of the EU's legislative and regulatory bodies to a democratic basis

- Replacement of the EU President by a Collegial Council based on the Swiss model, which represents the largest parliamentary groups. The latter takes decisions by consensus. Election occurs every four years by the Parliament and Senate, which is formed by the senators from the European regions close to the citizens (approx. 50-60).

- Drawing up a catalogue with clear competences of the EU, establishing an institution "Subsidarity Court" which keeps EU imperialism under control in order to find the right balance and to give the heterogeneous member states optimal development possibilities.

## Further measures to enhance democracy

- Limitation of the terms of office to two legislative periods

- Cooling off period for parliamentarians on leaving office. Three years for all ministers, state secretaries, and senior officials when the new activity is connected to their former subject area in politics.[104]

## 13.2 Transparency

Without a transparent policy (open government), citizens can only assume (very inadequately) whether the government complies with the democratic rules of the game. The slogan, "sunlight is the best disinfectant" underlines,

---

[104] Translated from: Gregor Hackmack, p. 44

that transparency is the best preventive measure against patronage, corruption, and other abuses.

A transparent policy also requires the use of clear language that reflects the issue as it is.

> "Social conflict is always first and foremost a battle for words. Whoever succeeds in introducing a term with a distorted meaning into the debate has already won half of the battle."
>
> -Paul Schreyer, Author[105]

## Transparency of the origin and use of money

- Establishment of a blockchain-based real-time register for party donations

- Conversion of the accounting of public bodies to a blockchain-based solution. This makes it easy to track who receives money, even if it is spread over several budget titles.

- Contract publication obligation for all contracts of the state with third parties. Contracts with an order volume of over 100,000 euros must have right of withdrawal of 30 days exists after the contract publication.[106]

- Conversion of the accounting of state-financed parties and their connected groups to a blockchain-based solution. This will create transparency with regard to party financing, allocations to individual members of parliament, the financing of parliamentary groups, and the financing of party-related foundations.

---

[105] Translated from: Paul Schreyer, Die Angst der Eliten – Wer fürchtet die Demokratie, p. 32

[106] Translated from: Gregor Hackmack, p. 49-50 and 93-94

**Measures to increase transparency**

- Establishment of a general transparency register. All public organizations must make documents (contracts, memos, etc.) publicly available on their own initiative.

- Establishment of a central unit for whistle blowers directly reporting to the constitutional court.

- Establishment of a mandatory lobby register. Lobbyists list with which budget, with what personnel, on whose behalf, and on which subject they influence politics.

- Establishment of a documented "legislative footprint" who gave input or otherwise influenced the creation of a draft bill or regulation etc.

- Rule to disclose all revenues of the parties in their annual reports.

- To 1,000 Euro exact publication of the extra income of the representatives.

- Blockchain-based log for access to personal data by the Federal Criminal Police Office or any other authority. Only access with registered proof of judicial authorization.

- No collaboration of paid lobbyists in ministries (e.g. pre-written laws).

**Conflicts of interest**

Potential conflicts of interest of representatives must be verifiable. The disclosure of their clients however, is categorically rejected for example, by members of parliament who also practice as lawyers. They refer to the lawyer's duty of confidentiality. In the case of lawyers, one must therefore rely on their word that they will not be influenced in their decision by the business with their clients. Without resorting to one of the many lawyers' jokes on the subject of morality, it can be said that this situation is not satisfactory.

But how is this possible without forcing lawyers to break their confidentiality? The process could look like this for all self-employed lawyers or those who have at least a 10% share or are a partner in their law firm:

- From a cumulative annual order threshold (value to be defined), members must enter their customers and assign them to one or more industries. These are registered with them as representative.

- Immediate encryption of all data before it is stored in the database.

- Hiring cataloguing and research experts who have a suitable key to decipher the names of the companies (without their connection to the representatives) and conduct research on the companies or individuals. The companies and persons will be identified according to industries and sectors. Every day, the experts receive far more anonymous cataloging requests than the number of new companies entered by the members of parliament. In this way, the actually relevant companies "disappear" in the mass of enquiries.

- Random checks of the cataloguing experts and recording of the error rate for the industry classification.

- Determination of potential conflicts of interest during the preparation of a law. If certain industries or sectors are influenced by the legislation, there is a conflict of interest due to a contractual relationship with them.

- Automated search of the database for members of parliament and sectors to identify a potential conflict of interest.

- Daily dispatch of an encrypted notification to all deputies. When this message is opened, it almost always indicates that there is nothing special. For some members of parliament however, there is a reference to the fact that they are not allowed to vote on a particular bill.

- Each legislation meeting is preceded by a written note. This states, that representatives with a conflict of interest with industries/sectors X and Y may not vote or have to abstain. This note shall be read before the vote on the law in Parliament.

- All bills must be voted on by name.

- Immediately after each vote, the conflicts of interest of the deputies who voted "yes" or "no" are compared with the subject of the vote and its restrictions. If a conflict arises, the member will be openly admonished by the chair and excluded from the meeting. The vote must be repeated without the representative concerned being present.

If the procedure outlined above is not legally possible, the relevant legislation should be adapted. Anyone who thinks of a better system is welcome to send me a proposal.


## 13.3 Media

As described in Chapter 7.5, the mass media perform their task as the "fourth power in the state" (to a very limited extent). Too often in recent years, media acted as advertiser for the German government. Too often, facts and opinions are not separated, and facts and events are not put into context. Too often, journalists see themselves as educators of their readers / listeners / viewers. Trust in the media has, to a large extent, been gambled away. According to the ARD (Germany's most important public media) media documentary in July 2016, 67 percent of viewers, readers, and listeners say that they have little or no trust in the media.[107]   The current scandals surroundding the price loaded reporter Claas Relotius,[108] who forged interviews to meet expectations and the infamous "ARD Framing Manual"[109] do nothing to restore trust.

This section should not be understood as a general critique of the media. Any journalist who upholds the principles of journalism and is committed to maintaining and winning room for critical journalism is an ally.

As Walter Lippmann remarked in his well-known book *Public Opinion*, the task of the media is not an easy one:

> "The function of news is to signalize an event, the function of truth is to bring to light the hidden facts and set them in relation to each other, and make a picture of reality on which men can act."

Journalism, especially German journalism, suffers from a false self-conception. Value-oriented journalism seems to follow an educational mission and patronize its readers. Too often, journalistic standards (at least two independent sources, also questioning the opposite side, clear separation of factual report and opinion, mentioning all important facts…, etc.) are ignored. And the result is published by the editorial staff anyway, because the news "fits into the narrative."


## News agencies as the invisible nerve center of the media

Due to the lack of resources and time pressure, most of the reports are taken over by the international news agencies: *Reuters, AFP, dpa, and AP*. Few of these reports are questioned or supplemented by research outside the

---

[107] Translated from: Jens Wernicke, p. 325, Daniela Rahn
[108] Spiegel: "Claas Relotius Affair: The Lessons we are drawing"
[109] Translated from: https://www.nachdenkseiten.de/?p=49466, Wer den Zustand der ARD beschönigt, wird ihre Glaubwürdigkeit noch weiter beschädigen

databases of the news agencies. "Ultimately, the dependence on global agencies creates a striking similarity in international reporting: from Vienna to Washington, our media often report on the same topics and even use the same formulations in many cases - a phenomenon that would otherwise be associated with 'guided media' in authoritarian countries."[110] What is not reported by these news agencies does not happen.

The result of a case study from October 2015 on the reporting by nine well-known daily newspapers in Germany, Austria, and Switzerland on Russia's intervention in the Syrian war:

> 55% News releases and reports from news agencies
>
> 23% Editorial reports based on agency material
>
> 9% came from background reports
>
> 10% opinions and guest comments (82% with interview partners close to NATO)
>
> 2% Interviews
>
> 0% from investigative research.[111]

Here lies an immense potential for influence, e.g. by state actors. According to the former head of the US news agency *AP*, the Pentagon employed more than 27,000 PR specialists in 2009. "High generals have threatened to ruin the AP and him if reporters continue to insist on their journalistic principles."[112]

---

[110] Translated from: Jens Wernicke, p. 159, Forschungsgruppe Propaganda
[111] Translated from: Jens Wernicke, p. 171 ff., Forschungsgruppe Propaganda
[112] Translated from: https://www.tagesanzeiger.ch/ausland/amerika/27000-PRBerater-polieren-Image-der-USA/story/20404513

## Pressure on journalists and tendency protection paragraph

The circulation of newspapers fell from 27 million in 1991 to only 15 million in 2016. Newspaper advertisements fell from 6.6 billion euros in 2000 to 2.5 billion euros in 2016. The consequences are the discontinuation of newspapers, savings, and outsourcing to freelance journalists. Gert Hautsch, author of the *Quarterly Reports on the German Media Industry* for the trade union ver.di: "Consequently the employed editors become blackmailable ... Everyone knows: if I am dismissed, I will hardly find another comparable position. Who dares to go against the political line of the publisher or his editor-in-chief?"[113]

This pressure is also exerted on individual journalists. If the article is not politically opportune, this can quickly lead to hostility from the editorial staff. It might also lead to a suggested move to another country, a ban on writing, or a labor court case. Many leading journalists take a different view. The media researcher Noam Chomsky, assumes a pre-selection and comments:

> "The decisive point is the following: These journalists would have long since lost their jobs if they hadn't proven long ago that nobody has to tell them what to write - because they will write the 'right thing' anyway. If they had followed the 'false' stories at the beginning of their career, they wouldn't even have gotten into the position where they can now 'say anything they want'...In other words, these journalists were already going through a process of socialization."[114]

A further complicating factor in Germany is the "tendency protection paragraph" in media employment law. "Tendenzschutz" is the protection of tendencies. This means the publisher has the right to determine the political

---

[113] Translated from: Jens Wernicke, p. 299, Gerd Hautsch
[114] Translated from: Jens Wernicke, p. 168-169, Forschungsgruppe Propaganda

tendency of his medium. The publisher may determine the political direction and oblige his editors and freelance journalists in a company agreement to produce texts, pictures, and films of a certain political point of view in a certain way. There is no right for editors to be journalistically and content-wise independent of the publisher.[115]

## Reducing the distance through fraternization

"You are specifically invited. You meet, and sometimes you are on a first-name basis. You exchange ideas…and at some point, the media person identifies himself with those who should actually be reported on critically. He or she thinks he belongs, feels very comfortable with it, and wants to prevent it from stopping."[116]

## Psychology Behind the shrinking Diversity of Opinions Through Political Correctness

"…They are not simply offered information. Rather, the information is linked to certain opinions that one should have about certain information. And these opinions now are linked to moral evaluations. So that if they do not represent certain opinions themselves, they automatically stand in the corner of evil…And that's exactly how the attitude journalism is formed, which scandalizes any dissenting opinion, and which also makes clear to everyone the price one has to pay if one wants to be non-conformist, if one wants to express a dissenting opinion. This price is getting higher and higher."[117]

---

[115] Translated from: https://de.wikipedia.org/wiki/Tendenzschutz
[116] Translated from: Jens Wernicke, p. 296, Gerd Hautsch
[117] Translated from: https://youtu.be/W2WkPolNDtI?t=1283, Wissensmanufaktur, Prof. Norbert Bolz: Der Journalist als Oberlehrer

The US-lawyer and vice president of the Mackinac Center for Public Policy, Joseph P. Overton, designed the following scale (Overton Window):

current policy - popular view - reasonable - acceptable - radical - unthinkable

"The formal freedom to say what you think does not mean much if you no longer dare to think what you are not allowed to say. Since in the long run it's too exhausting to think differently than you talk, most people think politically correct or at least a lot of people do. What does that actually mean? We are not actually afraid of having a wrong opinion, but we are afraid of standing alone with our opinion. That is what social psychologists call fear of isolation. And this fear of isolation governs our world. But those who fear the anger of others easily agree with the opinion of the clear majority, even if they actually know better. You silence yourself. That is the censorship that really counts...You silence yourself in order not to jeopardize your good reputation."[118]

"You repeat what you say. And what you say is not the opinion of the majority, but the opinion of well-articulated minorities. This is the starting point for a dynamic, which Elisabeth Nölle-Neumann analyzed many decades ago and which she gave the name "spiral of silence." And exactly this spiral of silence is used today by political correctness. What does the spiral of silence mean? Basically: Because minorities are often well articulated, and because they find resonance in the echo of the mass media, individuals believe that they are themselves in the minority and the others are the majority. And that is why they remain silent. So, they fall silent because they believe themselves to be in the minority, perhaps even as a radical minority. They think that the others are in the majority. But those are simply well articulated and have the loudspeakers of the mass media on their side. In the

---

[118] Translated from: https://youtu.be/W2WkPolNDtI?t=2081, Wissensmanufaktur, Prof. Norbert Bolz: Der Journalist als Oberlehrer

end this mechanism leads to minority rule; democracy is not the rule of the majorities, but the rule of well-articulated minorities."[119]

Prof. Bolz criticizes the so-called intellectuals: "Their power-protected, sentimental, moralizing discourse of political correctness uses ethics as a means of justification and puts any dissident in the media pillory. The realm of the mind today falls apart into the self-righteous and the intimidated."[120] The tools:

- Moralism (moralization makes discussion impossible and splits into good and evil)
- Language hygiene (politically correct language)
- Lazaret poetry (show pictures of crying, suffering children; a monster with a different opinion).

Prof. Bolz considers the use of the mechanisms mentioned above to be very dangerous: "The greatest danger for democracy is not the hatred of the radical losers, but the silence of the many who feel patronized by the paternalism of the media elite."[121]

## System criticism of the media

According to Professor Rainer Mausfeld, the entire media system "is structured economically and organizationally in such a way that it does not require any targeted personal control. Its conformity to the prevailing ideology already results from filter mechanisms that are a direct consequence

---

[119] Translated from: https://youtu.be/W2WkPolNDtI?t=2280, Wissensmanufaktur, Prof. Norbert Bolz: Der Journalist als Oberlehrer
[120] Translated from: https://youtu.be/W2WkPolNDtI?t=2760
[121] Translated from: https://youtu.be/W2WkPolNDtI?t=2990

of the structural economic power relations in which the media are embedded."[122]

David Goeßmann also doesn't see a conscious manipulation as the core problem: "In principle, journalists from media companies and broadcasters report what they have in front of their eyes, quite professionally and objectively. They do not do this in a vacuum, but within a very narrow ideological framework. As stated before, the media have an institutional side. This list works like a set of filters through which information and opinions pass. And these filters are designed so that not all information, opinions, backgrounds and voices have the same chance to pass. They don't receive the same attention - even if their relevance is essential for understanding events."[123]

## Fast food for media and the value of a story

Time pressure leads to the unchecked publication of articles that have already been prepared and forwarded by third parties. Empirical studies have shown that "nearly two thirds of all reports disseminated in the media are not independently researched but originate from the press offices of private and public institutions or PR agencies. They are offered to the media services as ready-made "snackable" articles. Eighty percent of all news in the media are based on only one source…the press office that circulated the report."[124]

According to the Polish journalist Ryszard Kapuscinski, "the value of information is no longer measured by its truth, but by its attractiveness. Above all, it must sell well. This now justifies almost any means: boulevardization, personalization, simplification, polarization, melodramatic-

---

[122] Translated from: Jens Wernicke, p. 139, Rainer Mausfeld
[123] Translated from: Jens Wernicke, p. 32, David Goeßmann
[124] Translated from: Jens Wernicke, p. 189, Jörg Becker

zation, and visualization of almost all topics are just catchwords for this. Proven journalistic standards such as care, intellectual independence, and fairness have a hard time."[125]

## Dependency of private media due to their business model

Private media must earn more money than they spend. Due to the internet and the almost-free availability of news and quality content, their business model of ad and reader subscription financing has dwindled. In addition, revenues from paid classified ads are also declining, as these are operated much more effectively by online providers. Many formats have abandoned their printed versions and are only available online. They try to finance themselves through income from the placement of advertising banners. Only a few quality media, such as the *Wall Street Journal*, have succeeded in attracting paying subscribers.

Just as in the print business, negative headlines sell better than positive ones due to the human psyche. As the saying goes: "If it bleeds it leads". It is about eyeballs and not the truth. Some media use particularly lurid headlines ("click bait") which lead to many visits to the article page. This website is then mercilessly paved with banners of the more pleasant or unpleasant blinking variety. This annoys the reader. After all, the user is just an accessory, since the main focus is on a potential earning of a whole cent of advertising revenue with his visit. As a reaction, users arm themselves with advertising blockers, which means that media earn even less.

All this makes the media very influenceable. They will carefully consider whether to report negatively on a large advertising customer. Journalistic independence ends with a crisis that threatens their existence. It also

---

[125] Translated from: Jens Wernicke, p. 305 f, Rainer Butenschön

strengthens the trend to present the development of the world in a rather negative light, although good progress has been made in most areas.[126]

We can still hope that media will find new business models that will bring them more in line with the interests of readers. New blockchain-based approaches such as Coil and Basic Attention Token (monthly subscription to all participating websites, micropayments after the time spent on the website) or the Oyster project (execution of small arithmetic operations as payment during reading time), are promising, but still have to prove themselves in reality. More traditional approaches such as the Swiss magazine *Republik* financed entirely by the readers are just as useful. Civil, a journalism network based on transparency and trust and owned by the community, is pursuing a different approach with a new reward model. $

## Media as another key to the success of democratization

Some social critics, such as Andreas Popp, see media as a decisive factor for successful social change. His "Plan B"[127] contains the media as one of its four building blocks. If nothing is changed in this field, the chances of real change decrease massively. Professor Reiner Mausfeld sees an opportunity for democratization through a re-politicization of society. He also considers the transformation of the media to be crucial.[128]

> "So, if we want to create a true democracy, we must radically reform the entire media system - especially in terms of its economic structure and its symbiotic networking with the economic and political centers

---

[126] https://www.ted.com/talks/steven_pinker_is_the_world_getting_better_or_worse_a_look_at_the_numbers, Ted Talk Steve Pinker: Is the world getting better or worse? A look at the numbers
[127] Translated from: https://www.wissensmanufaktur.net/plan-b/
[128] Translated from: Jens Wernicke, p. 153, Rainer Mausfeld

of power - in order to achieve comprehensive democratic control of the media."

The topic media is still very important, but it does not stem from the main idea of the party as grassroot democracy and transparency.

The Proxy Party stands for a transparent presentation of the facts and decision-making basis. In this way, it creates the most objective basis possible for anyone interested to be able to deal with topics, possible options for action, and their expected consequences. But the majority of the population will continue to inform themselves exclusively through the established media. Since these have a large influence, there is a potential danger that these will report less comprehensively and objectively and influence their readers/viewers/listeners in a "politically opportune" direction.

The following suggestions should not be seen in absolute terms. It should only serve as a basis for discussion; for more journalism and less "opinion-making." The following quote should not be taken literally, but should be thought-provoking:

> "Journalism is printing what someone else does not want printed. Everything else is public relations."
>
> -George Orwell, Author

## Public broadcasting corporations and fact checks for high-reach media

Some countries have a system with public broadcasting media that is either financed by taxpayer money or via direct levies from all citizens of the country.

The idea of a publicly financed broadcasting medium might seem strange to Americans, but it has some merit. The major argument in favor of publicly financed broadcasting is that these institutions would be focused on the neutral political education of the citizens. It would offer well-balanced, high-quality content to enable citizens to form their own opinion about topics. And this, would thus contribute to a functioning democratic community. This institution cannot be bought and cannot be influenced by ad dollars as it doesn't require ad revenue for financing.

Unfortunately, reality is not too close to this ideal. True independence was never achieved by any of these broadcasting mediums. In the following, I take a closer look at the British BBC and the German public broadcasting system.

A study[129] from the *Reuters Institute* took a closer look at eight European Public Service News organizations. It researched if the Public Service News is successfully closing the "Left-Right Reach Gap". The BBC and four other organizations scored favorably. The German system and two others have a left-leaning audience.

## GREAT BRITAIN

"The BBC domestic television channels do not broadcast advertisements, they are instead funded by a television license fee which TV viewers are required to pay annually."[130] Only their international programs are financed by advertisements.

Author Tom Mills pinpoints the missing independence of the BBC in an interview with openDemocracy:

> "The BBC has always been formally accountable to ministers for its operations. Governments set the terms under which it operates, they

---

[129] https://reutersinstitute.politics.ox.ac.uk/our-research/old-educated-and-politically-diverse-audience-public-service-news, p. 33
[130] https://en.wikipedia.org/wiki/BBC_Television

appoint its most senior figures who, in the future will be directly involved in day-to-day managerial decision making, and they set the level of the license fee, which is the BBC's major source of income. So that's the context within which the BBC operates, and it hardly amounts to independence in any substantive sense."[131]

In his book *The BBC: Myth of a Public Service*, Tom Mills clearly states that the BBC has been leaning towards the government position:

"Throughout its existence, the BBC has been in thrall to those in power. This was true in 1926 when it stood against the workers during the General Strike, and since then the Corporation has continued to mute the voices of those who oppose the status quo: miners in 1984; anti-war protesters in 2003; those who offer alternatives to austerity economics since 2008."

A good example of how the game plays out when the reporting conflicts with government interests, was in a reporting about the Iraq War:

"The Iraq War was another area where scholarly research found that the BBC was more favourable to the government and its supporters, compared with other broadcasters…When the Blair government then attacks the BBC, it's true that the BBC leadership stands firm, and that's certainly commendable. But what then ultimately happens is that the chair and director general are both forced to resign, and the BBC publicly apologises to the government – a government that let's not forget, launched an illegal war on a plainly false pretext."[132]

---

[131] https://www.opendemocracy.net/en/ourbeeb/bbc-is-neither-independent-or-impartial-interview-with-tom-mills/
[132] https://www.opendemocracy.net/en/ourbeeb/bbc-is-neither-independent-or-impartial-interview-with-tom-mills/

Unfortunately, this biased reporting seems to be ongoing when you take a look at the BBCs role in the Brexit vote and its very much one-sided role in favor of the remain side.[133]

## GERMANY

The organizational framework for the German public broadcast system was modeled with the BBC in mind. The supervisory bodies appointing the most senior figures are made up of representatives of the socially relevant groups. These include political parties, trade unions, social associations, churches, etc. The political parties usually account for no more than 30% of the seats. The system is financed by direct levies on all individuals (86% of the budget). They are only allowed to broadcast 20 min. of advertisements before 8 pm.[134] Among others, the association "standing viewer conference of public media" criticizes the fact that public broadcasters often disregard these standards. The following text sharply criticizes ARD's reporting on the Greek crisis:

> "We accuse ARD of having overdone the audience with disinformation, false statements, and omissions of important information over weeks and months, contrary to the stipulations of the Interstate Broadcasting Treaty. ARD's coverage of Greece - explicitly from the *Tagesschau* (THE German prime time news broadcast) and 'Tagesthemen' - was one-sided, conformist with the government, manipulative, hostile, slanderous and in parts downright absurd because of its boulevard-style narrative. Through the inflationary spread of national stereotypical clichés in connection

---

[133] https://www.spiked-online.com/podcast-episode/people-desperately-want-their-vote-to-matter/ min. 41:37

[134] Translated from: https://de.wikipedia.org/wiki/%C3%96ffentlich-rechtlicher_Rundfunk#Grundlagen

with the Greek national debt, lower instincts such as envy, hatred, cynicism, and open racism were awakened among the German population, and discord was sown among the European neighbors." [135]

It is not without reason that many books, including those by former insiders, disapprove of the uncritical attitude of the German public media towards the positions of the government and NATO. The case of the former ZDF editor-in-chief Nikolaus Brender, who's contract was not prolonged, led to debates on the political influence on public service broadcasting. [136]

The following ideas should be discussed. As with the rest of the book, these are only initial suggestions and I am very open to other solution-oriented suggestions.

- Independent, objective reporting, public broadcasters with a clear political educational mandate. Focused on well-balanced information, clearly separated presentation of facts, and their prudential assessment. Independence here means in particular that politics has no say in the filling of positions. Key positions should be newly filled as quickly as possible.

- Unbundling of the relationship networks between politics and public broadcast institutions.

- Establish a decentralized totally independent body that defines journalistic standards (clear separation of report and opinion, at least two independent citable sources, balance of research and consultation of the other side, assessment of truthfulness, etc.). At

---

[135] Translated from: Jens Wernicke, p. 265, Maren Müller
[136] Translated from: https://de.wikipedia.org/wiki/%C3%96ffentlich-rechtlicher_Rundfunk#Grundlagen

the start, exclusive occupation by journalists without current party ties. The appointment of leadership should be made, for example, by journalists well known for their balanced critical examination of government activities. The funding is provided through a levy on the reduced public broadcast contribution and amounts to 1% of the reduced contribution.

- A warning of false facts can be handed in by anyone - source references for the correct information or an argumentation of the discovered inconsistencies have to be included. The whistleblowers must also be evaluated. This counteracts excessive demands on the system. The inputs are processed in the order of their potential importance:

  Reach of the medium * Quality assessment of the claim maker The quality level of the claim maker is evaluated in such a way that he can build up a reputation. A quality assessor proven by his history has approximately ten times the weighting of a new assessor.

- For the introduction of the system, the processes must first be tested on some leading media formats such as *Tagesschau* (German prime time news) and then extended to all leading public media. Private sector media can voluntarily join the system ahead of time. At a later stage, the system should be mandatory for media with a certain reach.

- Corrections must be made on the same page in (print medium), in the article (online medium), or at the end of the program (television). The size of the text or the length of the video contribution depends on the original contribution.

- In the case of print and online media, the number of factual errors in the last year must be shown on the title page under the logo and in the case of videos in the start sequence / intro. A kind of reputation point system.

- Disclosure of the research of the fact check institution including all sources that contributed significantly to the evaluation.

- Linking the bonuses of the public media leadership to the assessment of compliance with these journalistic standards.

- Public grants to develop technologies and solutions that verify photos, videos, and audio recordings as authentic (location, time, integrity of material). Open source the technology.

Legal framework

- Arms producing or selling companies are not allowed to directly or indirectly own shares in media companies. This is also valid for companies whom have shares in these companies.

- Reduction of the participation of parties in media companies to one that has to use the party abbreviation clearly in its name, e.g. "SPD Media." Sub-ownerships are not permitted. Or, the following regulations:

  - Disclosure of the ownership structure of media companies above a certain range: Mention of the last beneficiaries in the imprint from 5%. Mention directly under the logo from 25%. Of course, this also applies to parties.

- Abolition of any laws or other instruments that counteract freedom of expression

- No new instruments that want to sanction critical reporting. Objective criticism should always be welcome!

  - Amendment of passages of the UN Migration Pact.

  - No EU "truth ministry" that can cut EU party funding for parties working with disinformation. This will be decided by EU authorities, which will be "prosecutors, judges, and executioners" at the same time. It is for the fear that EU authorities will cut out parties with unpopular opinions from their funding.[137]

• Reversal of the EU copyright reform and the associated upload filters, which would lead, a filtering by central providers. This creates a central point for content monitoring, and if necessary, deactivation. The German model it was copied from clearly showed that this is dysfunctional, hostile to innovation and competition, and runs counter to the interests of internet users.

## 13.4 Complementary topics

The core issues of democracy and transparency form the necessary basis. On this basis, we can work together to find solutions to the major challenges facing our society. Based on the core issues and within the framework of the processes that ensure democracy, the new party must develop approaches to the challenges of our time. The aim should be to broaden the choice of parties with a genuine alternative, which differs greatly in two key points:

• more trustworthy (provably more democratic and transparent)

• a bold vision with solutions to the great challenges of our time, rather than marginal changes

---

[137] Translated from: https://kenfm.de/tagesdosis-26-10-2018-merkel-und-eu-wollen-wahrheitsministerium/

## Identify common topics

You can compare the Proxy Party with a white canvas waiting to be painted. The canvas itself sets the frame with its form (transparency and democracy). The painter should wear clear glasses (media) so that he can judge his environment and the results of his work on the canvas as objectively as possible. The party members must agree on the theme of the picture, the materials used, and the atmosphere of the picture. They co-operatively design the work.

The party should above all express the will of its members and continue to develop thematically. In the course of time, further focal points will develop.

The party will focus on issues where consensus has been reached:

- Discussions are focused to find common ground and not discrepancy.
- A minimum will be set; universal values and goals for everyone.
- With a 2/3 or ¾ majority, an agreed, basic consensus can be included in the extended party program.
- As soon as the agreement on a topic falls below 60%, this is taken out of the extended party program.
- The party, and thus also the representatives, focus on the basic consensus agreed in the party core program and the extended party program and try to push this.

## What issues should the vision cover?

The current system has resulted in many heavily indebted states having to spend an ever-increasing proportion of their tax revenues on interest. The financial crisis of 2007/2008 has accelerated this process and further reduced the creditworthiness of many countries. This is only sustainable for some countries because the central banks are operating at or close to zero interest rates. The crisis to be expected in the coming years will increase these debts considerably. At the same time, the ageing of society is putting pressure on social security funds.[138] The financial scope for social and environmental programs will be further reduced, leaving even more people behind. The pressure to privatize state property to create financial relief in the short term is increasing.

The flood of cheap money has created huge bubbles in the real estate and stock markets. The resulting rise in rents, especially in large cities, is a heavy burden for many people whose job security, especially due to automation, continues to decline.

Although more than three trillion US dollars have flowed into developing countries since 1960,[139] their situation does not seem to have improved markedly, with a few exceptions. We face huge worldwide challenges in the environmental and in society. The shortfall in the social sector and the overshoot in the environmental sector can be seen very clearly in the doughnut model that was created by Kate Raworth and Christian Guthier.[140] The existing economic system leads to a "redistribution from bottom to top, from south to north and from the public to the private sector."[141] The state was "largely transformed into a redistributive and subsidized state for the economically strong and a surveillance state for the economically weak."[142] In many countries, the lowest income classes experienced real wage cuts.

---

[138] https://www.economicshelp.org/blog/8950/society/impact-ageing-population-economy/

[139] Translated from: http://bogner-verlag.de/geldfluesse-in-der-entwicklungszusammenarbeit-seit-1960

[140] https://www.weforum.org/agenda/2017/04/the-new-economic-model-that-could-end-inequality-doughnut/ and https://www.kateraworth.com/doughnut/

[141] Translated from: Rainer Mausfeld, Position 2777

[142] Translated from: Rainer Mausfeld, Position 2741

Wages, which rose only slightly, could not compensate for rising prices, especially rent. In Germany the lower 40% of wage laborers saw a decrease from 1995 to 2015.[143] The laborers in the lowest 20% saw a decrease of 7% in this timeframe. According to the Pew Research Center, the lower half of the American wage laborers basically didn't see a raise since 2000.[144] Further results of our economic order: more than 46 million slaves worldwide.[145] Over 800 million people are starving, several million starve every year.[146] The tension between America and Russia (as well as America and China), are increasing and prominent voices in America speak of the possibility of a limited use of nuclear weapons.

In short, it is foreseeable that simply continuing will lead to a catastrophe and that the changes proposed by most parties will not suffice.

The following is a list of what I consider to be the central and most urgent questions we as a society should ask ourselves and find solutions for:

- How do we provide billions of people with a livelihood and meaning if technological progress destroys far more jobs than it creates?

- How do we reduce poverty so that everyone can lead a dignified life?

- How do we raise money for the elderly with fewer workers and far more older people?

- How can we prepare for a global financial crisis?

- How can we prepare for a Euro crisis?

---

[143] Translated from: https://www.boeckler.de/pdf/atlas_der_arbeit_2018.pdf, Atlas der Arbeit, p. 14

[144] https://www.pewresearch.org/fact-tank/2018/08/07/for-most-us-workers-real-wages-have-barely-budged-for-decades/

[145] https://www.weforum.org/agenda/2019/01/fact-check-how-many-people-are-enslaved-in-the-world-today/

[146] https://www.welthungerhilfe.org/hunger/

- How can we make a decisive contribution to improving the situation in developing countries quickly and sustainably, so that people no longer need to immigrate to Europe / the US in large numbers?
- How can we massively reduce environmental degradation?
- How can we prevent "The New Cold War" from becoming hot?
- Do we need a modification of our economic system to positively influence the above-mentioned points?

List of the main underlying factors:

- Technological progress
- Demographic development: ageing society
- Our economic system
- Our monetary system with the Euro as the single European currency
- Economic and development aid policy
- Environmental policy
- Geopolitics and foreign policy

Some approaches in the form of questions:

1. How can technological progress be used more effectively to achieve a significant improvement in the quality of life of all people, including those who are not in official employment or have already left the labor force, without weakening the entrepreneurial forces that generate these innovations?

2. How should an economic and monetary system be designed so that as many people as possible experience a noticeable improvement in their quality of life?

3. How should fair trade be designed and how should it be complemented by an effective development aid policy so that the

quality of life in developing countries can be significantly and sustainably improved?

4. How can an environmental policy ensure a massive reduction in the depletion of resources and the accumulation of toxins, without limiting points 1-3 too much? To what extent can technological innovations contribute to this?

5. How can we contribute to a de-escalation of the political situation with a new foreign policy?

## Summary

Grassroot democracy and transparency: The Proxy Party is above all a grassroot democratic party. In order to create and maintain a genuine grassroots democracy, processes and decisions must be transparent.

Media: The media have an important role to play in shaping political opinion. Therefore, the complete independence of the public broadcast media must be achieved. The contributions of high-circulation media should be independently checked by a decentralized organization. Evaluators also have to be quality checked; evaluation weight depending on the quality of their previous work.

Core Program and Extended Party Program: To emphasize the importance of the above topics Democracy and Transparency, they are written into a party core program. All political plans will be included in the extended party program if they receive sufficient approval. This can be changed at any time. This distinction is made in order not to restrict the party thematically from the very beginning. The potential party members should be offered a reform party but asides, just "a blank canvas." Ideally, the supplementary topics should be determined when the party has reached a certain size and thus approximately represents the population.

# 14. Electoral program derived from the core themes

The two core issues of "Democracy" and "Transparency" give rise to many potential election campaign issues. It remains to be determined which individual issues can best be communicated and seem the most attractive for voters. These topics should be given priority in elections. The following list can surely be extended.

## Democracy

Structure

- Establishing the democratic separation of powers. The three pillar of democracy: executive, legislative, and judiciary, must become independent of each other.

Elections, referendums, referenda, etc.

- Introduction of nationwide referendums and popular initiatives. Obligatory addition of planning cells, which consist of randomly selected representative citizens (see Chapter 13.1). They help voters find their way by providing a concise, easily understandable citizens' report.

- Direct election of the heads of the Federal and State Audit Offices, the heads of the public broadcasting corporations, the heads of the Federal States and the Federal President.

- Change of the election procedure to a ranked choice election to give the small parties better chances to get over the 5% hurdle.

- Introduction of an option "none of the parties is eligible for me to vote" on the ballot paper.

## Party financing

- Banning of corporate donations. No hidden financing through advertising in party newspapers or stands at party conferences or the like. Restriction of private donations to $5,000 per person per year. Conversion of party financing to vouchers for citizens, e.g. $100 for each election (like the Presidential candidate Andrew Yang proposes[147] as democracy dollars. These are delivered as five $20 vouchers. Unused vouchers go in a fund for election system improvement projects as proposed by Lawrence Lessig. Lessig also proposes to hand each candidate additional funds to run for office if this candidate (a) pledges to forgo other kind of contributions and (b) achieves to attract a predefined amount of voucher money.[148]

- Laws for the financing of the parties and/or the delegates (deciding on their own behalf) come into power only in the next legislative period.

---

[147] https://www.yang2020.com/policies/democracydollars/
[148] Lawrence Lessig, They don't Represent Us: Reclaiming Our Democracy, Pos. 2504

- Exclusive use of the employees of the representatives for parliamenttary work, instead of party work. Clear instruction of the Parliament to the employees paid by it and effective control.

## Parliament

- Transfer of the preparation of legislative papers to an independent policy assessment department that prepares each case for/ against changes of laws incl. an internal group that is vetting factuality, reason and balance. "This would ensure that the debates improve in quality, accuracy and accountability. That is, for each new law, independently create a publicly available case for and against, based on vetted contributions from all interested, including any costs and risks of change. Then have all of our legislators take the time in parliament to hear the vetted evidence and reasoning within those cases and make an informed and well considered collective decision."[149]
- Allocation of speaking rights and time by the Members and not by the chairmen of political groups.
- Banning of the obligation to follow your political group (whip).
- Banning of partial donation of the salary of representatives to their party.
- Tightening of the laws so that a minimum number of deputies must be present during votes. Very narrow definition of exceptions and explicit approval by the chairman of the assembly required.

---

[149] Tony Bracks, Solving for Democracy, p. 241

- Banning of ad-hoc votes. Very narrow definition of exceptions for an accelerated voting procedure, in order not to undermine the democratic control weights, and explicit approval by the Chairman of the Assembly required.

- All thematic votes in Parliament should be roll-call votes.

- Automatic single sunset clauses for all changes in law. The results of the change have to be measured against the expected effects. The measurement has to adhere to a predefined framework. If ever possible a change has to be trialed first with a thorough evaluation of its effects before it is rolled out to the whole nation.

## Party power expansion stop

- Limitation of the term of office of politicians to a maximum of two terms.

- Three years' cooling period for parliamentarians leaving office and moving to business.

- No additional official posts granted one year after the election and one year before the next official election date.

- The proportion of party members in the population determines the maximum number of party members that can be appointed to public offices in the public bodies on a city/county/state/federal level.

## Strengthen freedom of expression

- Abolish all laws that counteract freedom of expression.

- Defense against new instruments that seek to sanction critical journalism. Objective criticism should always be welcome. Examples:
  - Amendment of passages of the UN Migration Pact

- Stop plans for a "truth ministry" of the EU, which can then shorten funding for unpopular parties.

## Transparency

Publicly available information

- Conversion of public sector accounting to a publicly accessible blockchain-based accounting system.
- Changeover of the accounting of state-financed parties: Best to use a blockchain-based publicly accessible accounting system. At least: set up a real-time blockchain-based register for party donations
- Establishment of a general publicly available transparency register
- Introduction of a binding lobby register in which lobbyists list: with which budget, with what personnel, on whose behalf, and on which topics they influence politics. Clear definitions of who must register as a lobbyist
- Introduction of an official list of meetings with lobbyists (attendees, topics, time)
- Exact publication of the additional income of representatives
- Blockchain-based log for access to personal data by the police or other institutions only with proof of judicial authorization. Anonymous disclosure of compliance with legal processes.

## Reduce influence

- Lobbyist can talk with politicians, but they can't give them money.
- Paid lobbyists can't work in ministries
- Establishment of a register of elected representatives' conflicts of interest

### Media

- Abolition of politics filling positions in public media institutions

- Reduction of the participation of parties in media companies to one which must clearly bear the party abbreviation in its name, e.g. "SPD Media"

- Disclosure of the ownership structure of media companies above a certain range. Last beneficiaries have to be mentioned in the imprint from 5%, and directly under the logo from 25%. Ban of direct or indirect ownership by organizations that produce or sell arms.

### Other topics

- Open analysis and discussion of the political challenges. Moral arguments should only be discussed after the collection of facts and mechanisms of action. In case of doubt, the so-called "political correctness" has to be put aside, since solutions must take precedence over sensitivities. This is particularly the case when facts are ignored, or solutions are blocked.

This first collection of topics can of course, be expanded. It is important to ensure that the party has a clear profile.

# 15. Software systems for the Proxy Party

The current political system is hopelessly outdated. It does not use the new technologies and thus misses the opportunity to reach a higher level of democratic representation:

> "We are 21st century residents interacting with institutions
> created in the 19th century based on 15th century technology."
> -Pia Mancini, Democracy Earth Foundation

The system used by the Proxy Party must have some important features:

## 15.1 Security

- Open source: The source code of the system must be well documented and open source and must be understood by expert third parties.

- Access: The system must be accessible to everyone.

- Understandable: The choice options must be understood by everyone.

- Auditable: The options and their results must be verifiable and comprehensible.

- Software independence: An undiscovered change or error in the software must not lead to undiscovered changes or an error in the result of the choice.

The system must be as resistant as possible to the usual types of attack:

**Client side** (PC, notebook, smartphone, tablet…, etc.), i.e. the device on which the voter votes:

- Prevention of blackmail (the voter must not be able to provide any proof of his decision to vote)
- Protection against theft of login data
- Protection against phishing attacks
- Protection from web pages that pretend to be the party's website and pretend to have voted to the voter

**Server Side** (computers on which the system is running):

- Protection against Denial of Service attacks (DDos) to paralyze the service by flooding it with requests
- Protection against attacks by party members (insiders) or a service provider
- Protection against attacks by state actors

The new blockchain technology offers good approaches that can be used for a secure voting system. You can massively reduce, if not eliminate, server-side vulnerabilities. Every voter can check the correct inclusion of his vote himself. Some blockchain-based voting systems such as DemocracyEarth's Sovereign[150] system, are already available. The aim of this is to combine the greatest possible legitimacy with a simultaneous strengthening of the votes

---

[150] https://www.democracy.earth/

that are best informed.  Other systems are still under development and should be available soon.

## 15.2 Member authentication

Authentication is the critical component of the system. The party must ensure that each member is a natural person and only has one vote. Most likely it also has to check that the member is citizen of the city or state and has according voting rights.

There is no simple solution. A central solution is too vulnerable as it can be hacked. The best solution would be a decentralized solution combined with an official sign-off from a public authority for the information that can be found on an Identity Card and the eligibility to vote etc.

This is a very complex problem with no 100% solution in sight.

The most promising solution I came across up so far is described in a white paper[151] from Nicole Immorlica, Matthew O. Jackson, and Glen Weyl, that takes "Intersectional Identities" as a basis for the required proof. Their work refers back to the social reality of pre-formal identity. Identity then was a network of interpersonal direct or indirect knowledge about other persons. From the point of view of the authors, the crucial aspects of identity are redundancy, sociality and intersectionality:

> Redundancy: A person is uniquely defined by a set of features and past interactions. Even a subset of this unique set is sufficient to identify her. This implies that an individuum only has to give away a small part of her identity to authenticate herself. Identity theft is much harder to pull off than in the current central systems.

---

[151] https://papers.ssrn.com/sol3/papers.cfm?abstract_id=3375436

Sociality: Most of the data that uniquely defines a person is by its nature shared with others and known by others. This starts with the date of birth known by your parents and the doctor and nurses but is also valid for working with co-workers, in person discussions etc. This implies that normally "it is usually sufficient for that individual to use preexisting social sharing of data, thereby largely avoiding compromises of privacy or security."[152]

Intersectionality: The individual can in large parts be seen "as intersection of the social groups with whom the constituents of her identity are shared".[153] This enables the individual to rely on a range of different social connections to avoid making any individual or group a central chokepoint.

This approach can be combined with physical meetings to sign other individuals' cryptographic keys that serve as a proxy for identity. "Keys with many trusted signatures are themselves trusted and can be used as proof of identity."[154] The more facts a key signed off that later are deemed to be useful and truthful, the more additional trustworthiness is accumulated by this key.

Local meetings of party members of the Proxy Party can be used to link a name, citizenship and a location to a cryptographic key. A hash function that transforms the original data into an alphanumeric code that changes very noticeably with the smallest changes to the original would enable the detection of double entries as member of the Proxy Party. The process of signing of person data as seen on an official document can be split up in several steps. This avoids that a "stranger" sees the complete data on your

---

[152] Nicole Immorlica, Matthew O. Jackson, Glen Weyl, Verifying Identity as a Social Intersection, p. 2
[153] Nicole Immorlica, Matthew O. Jackson, Glen Weyl, p. 2
[154] Nicole Immorlica, Matthew O. Jackson, Glen Weyl, Verifying Identity as a Social Intersection, p. 6

identity card.

Some other interesting concepts that are useful as a base for decentralized identities are mentioned in a tweet[155] by Santi Sieri co-founder of Democracy.Earth:

- https://www.humanitydao.org/ with Twitter based profiles as proof secured on the blockchain.

- https://kleros.io that randomly elects jurors that verify videos of candidate IDs.

- https://idena.io synchronous events held over the entire network where participants are required to solve Turing tests that are hard for machine learning systems to solve.

- Anonymous Hardware, a proof of human mining device, that constantly delivers data like GPS data and heartrate.

## 15.3 Features as a voting system and coordination platform

The system must be extendable and have the following functionalities, among others, so that all necessary areas are covered:

- Member administration
    - Identity system
    - Membership fee administration (incl. exemption)
    - Role and rights system incl. expert bonus system
- Reputation system that recognizes and incentives behavior that contributes to the commons of the party
- Efficient topic identification

---

[155] https://twitter.com/santisiri/status/1182594365757149184

- Inclusion of new topics incl. creation of structured topic proposals
- Structured collection of proven facts and influencing factors and quality assurance
- Questions and discussions
- Voting on topics (gradual admission and involvement of more members)
- User exclusion mechanisms in case of violation

• Preparation of elections

- Preparation of the topic template (intro, facts, mechanisms, pros, cons, recommendations)
- Discussion of the topic template
- Release of the discussion template as decision basis according to threshold value (expert opinions account for 50% of the weighting)
- Evaluation of the participants (expert, normal participant), how satisfied they are with the topic (all important facets correctly presented, fair weighted presentation of the topic)

• Delegation system and elections

- Option to give votes from -1 up to +1 in 0.1 increments or 0.25 increments
- Delegation of votes for subject areas or individual votes
- A system to connect votes to decisions when delegated to a group
- Indication of how the delegate or his/her delegate has currently voted (the uncertainty about the potential further delegation of the vote does not violate voting secrecy)

- User can overwrite his vote at any time (until the last minute)
  - Election time restriction
  - Blockchain based
- Analysis of the election
  - Verification that the integrity of the vote has been maintained
  - Counting according to a pre-defined procedure
  - Determination of the election result
  - Verification, if the integrity of the vote counting was maintained according to the specified procedure
- Allocation of voting shares to elected representatives according to their own preferences and the distribution of the member votes (minimal difference from the personal choice of the representatives)
- Coordination of active party members
  - Expert profiles
  - Limitation of the number of text for contributions per user
  - System to rate users according to their valuable contributions and then allow them more text volume
  - Calendar
  - File repository
  - Further suggestions: see Piratenwiki[156]
- Activation of passive members
  - Notification of new relevant topics
  - Notification of successes, updates, etc.

---

[156] In German: https://wiki.piratenpartei.de/Hauptseite

- Invitation to local meetups
- Invitation to elections

The Pirate Party has already done very good work in this area (Piratenwiki, Liquid Democracy). Sebastian Jabbusch has written a master's thesis on experiences with liquid democracy.[157]

Some interesting systems, which are already part of the requirements outlined above:

- https://liqd.net/en/software
- Sovereign by https://democracy.earth
- Votorola[158]
- https://www.agora.vote
- https://aragon.org
- https://dcentproject.eu
- https://commonsstack.org[159]
- inilab.ch
- https://blog.colony.io
- https://nativeproject.one
- https://pol.is/home
- https://electric.vote
- https://consider.it

---

[157] German source: https://www.sebastianjabbusch.de/wp-content/uploads/2011/10/Liquid-Democracy-in-der-Piratenpartei-Eine-Neue-Chance-fur-die-innerparteiliche-Demokratie-im-21-Jahrhundert-By-Sebastian-Jabbusch.pdf
[158] German: https://wiki.piratenpartei.de/Liquid_Democracy/Votorola
[159] https://medium.com/giveth/introducing-the-commons-stack-scalable-infrastructure-for-community-collaboration-6886eb97413e

- https://holochain.org with some implementations like https://www.hylo.com and https://www.sacred.capital

Since the ideas for the system evolve faster than I could write them down in a book, the current status of the sketch of the system can be found on my website upgradingdemocracy.com.

You may be astounded to hear that a blockchain-based voting system is already in use by Jackson county as a vote-by-mobile option. The system is provided by Voatz.[160]

## Summary

The Proxy Party's system must be secure. This is the only way to ensure the legitimacy of the decisions taken via this platform.

The system must be scalable and enables the efficient interaction of many thousands, if not hundreds of thousands of users. In addition to the usual functionalities of a collaboration platform, the system must enable the following very efficiently:

- Suggest topics
- Decide on the importance of the topics
- Create topic decision templates
- Collect facts and cause-effect relationships and decentralized fact check
- Discuss topics aiming at maximum increase in knowledge for participants incl. reputation system
- Prepare elections

---

[160] https://mailtribune.com/news/top-stories/jackson-county-offers-vote-by-mobile

- Hold elections (incl. Liquid Democracy voting delegation)
- Analysis of elections
- Allocate the results of the elections to the representatives of the party

# 16. Questions about the Proxy Party

**Grassroot democracy = they just talk and achieve nothing**

A grassroots democratic party continuously coordinates with its members. This gives it a particularly high degree of legitimacy. This is good and ensures that the party leadership does not detach itself from its base. Such a party can only make a difference if it does not get bogged down in fundamental discussions. Otherwise it is mainly concerned with itself and, in extreme cases, blocks almost all of its work. I have already described the processes in more detail in Chapter 12.

As a clear directive, a healthy mix of quality and efficiency in policymaking must be put at the forefront. A good system must, among other things, cover four important points:

- It must focus on maximizing the knowledge gain for participants. It has to sort out questionable material, put information into context, and reveal mechanisms.

- It must encourage experts so that they contribute their knowledge (even the uncomfortable) undisturbed.

- For the benefit of all, it must moderate people who tend to focus their presentation on their ego instead of the topic and thereby waste the time of other participants.

- It must rein in characters who, by their brash nature and ego, intimidate other participants and thus suppress potential good contributions.

The above points are mainly achieved through discussion rules and a limitation of the activities of the members in the forums. They are also achieved by quality assurance.

As soon as the discussion on a topic exceeds a certain limit, the participants can only contribute a certain number of words (technically: number of characters). This personal, topic-related limitation, is only extended if enough other contributors rate the contributions as "valuable for discussion." Thus, the work is more fact-oriented and focused on the gain in knowledge.

In an extreme case, some "troublemakers" might try to get involved in the party just to undermine its work and keep them engaged with itself.

## Does everything have to be coordinated with the basis?

No. Not all topics have to be coordinated with all members. This is very inefficient and would only lead to the party officials being overloaded and almost all members being overwhelmed.

Most people have neither the time nor the interest to deal with all current political issues and to form an opinion on each of them. They like to delegate this responsibility to representatives. This is the major reason why we have a representative democracy with deputies representing the electorate.

The Proxy Party should be aware of this fact and should not overburden its members.

The party will have to decide on the issues it will vote on. These definitely include the following votes:

- Inclusion in the party's core program

- Inclusion in the extended party program
- Staff elections

For additional votes, it should be clarified beforehand in the interests of efficiency whether a vote is required on the subject:

- The party leadership must inform ahead of time about upcoming issues.

- If any of the issues raised by the party leadership is found by the members to be "not worth voting on," the party base need not vote. The party leadership may at any time release issues for voting by itself. Members may also propose their own topics.

- If the topic does not reach the minimum participation of the eligible voters ("interest hurdle"), e.g. 5%, as well as a simple majority of these, then the basis will not vote on the topic. Since delegated votes also count, the hurdle would be very easy to overcome.

The proposed system would be very flexible. The two extremes would be as follows:

If the trust in the party leadership is very high or the commitment of the party members very low, the Proxy Party acts practically like a normal party. The party officials determine the direction and the votes. From a technical point of view, this corresponds to the delegation of the votes of all members to the group "party leaders." The important difference: If there is no confidence in the party leadership on a subject, the party members can take the lead at any time and obtain a vote at the party member level. They can be sure that their votes will not only be heard, but that these will also be reflected in the way members vote.

If trust in the party leadership is low or the commitment of the party members is very high, many issues are decided at the level of the members.

Unlike other parties, elected representatives do not just assume what their party members want, but ask them and vote accordingly.

There should be a paragraph in the party's statutes which stipulates that the level of this percentage hurdle must be voted on every six months. This can be done within the framework of a permanent general meeting. All the members can regularly consider whether the party officials and the members use their rights wisely or whether this percentage should be amended.

Topics that have not yet been prepared pose a challenge. For these, there is not yet a sound basis for a decision which would enable the members to prepare themselves quickly and neutrally. A distinction must be made here:

- The quality of active submissions of topics to the Bundestag or the regional parliament must be guaranteed. The active submission can only take place when the decision basis has reached a high degree of maturity and the majority of the basis decides in favor of a proposal.

- The hurdle can be lowered when voting on laws and topics introduced by others. If the preparation time is too short, there should be a tendency to reject the proposal, if only to point out a lack of democracy. However, the basis can also simply rely on its representatives who, guided by the party program, will vote according to their consciences.

Not every topic is equally important. Especially at the beginning, a not clear-cut thematic focus leads to a dilution of the focus and the profile of the party. This would lead to a decrease in the quality of the work. If the party develops the ambition to work on far more topics, then it will be important to win many specialists and active members to prepare and discuss topic. The more active members that can be won over, the more topics can be worked on.

## How does the Proxy Party vote internally?

The objection to the usual electoral procedure, in which one person has one vote, is the possible "suppression of minorities by the majority." The other end of the spectrum can be described as "loud minorities dominating."

It should be considered to use quadratic voting.[161] In this case, each voter receives a voting point budget with the same number of voting points and can use these for all votes. He is allowed to cast several votes in one vote. However, these become increasingly expensive:

> The allocation of one vote costs 1x1= 1 voting point
>
> two votes cost 2x2= 4 voting points
>
> three votes cost 3x3= 9 voting points, etc.

This type of voting allows the strength of the voter's point of view to be expressed and it is very costly to dominate a vote. People committed to a topic are generally also more interested in it. They are better informed about it. So, this voting procedure should also lead to better results in purely factual terms. If votes are delegated, they receive less voting weight in a quadratic voting procedure. For example, if a member has been delegated with nine votes and has his own vote, his votes only count as three. Votes from voters who vote themselves or pass on their vote(s) to delegates who are not so "popular" are thus more valuable.

When voting for staff, the Coombs election procedure described in Chapter 11.3 should be followed. If necessary, a system should also be chosen in which each candidate is given a vote, e.g. strong rejection/ rejection/ neutral/ approval/ strong approval) with the values -3/ -1/ 0/ +1 / +3. The winner will be determined by adding up the total number of points.

---

[161] https://en.wikipedia.org/wiki/Quadratic_voting and https://collectivedecisionengines.com/index.html

## How does the Proxy Party differ from a normal party?

The Proxy Party

... is organized on the basis of grassroots democracy and also includes the most important right of the member of parliament.

... obliges the elected representative to vote as determined by the party base. This is only an approximation of the will of the voters but is much closer to it than the usual approach of a party.

... does not ignore the dissenting votes of its members but reflects them in the vote.

... is therefore more relaxed in the internal discussion, since it is not a question of necessarily having to achieve a 50% majority.

... can function like a normal party if all members delegate their votes to the party leadership, but has a grassroots democratic corrective. The member can "take back" the vote at any time, i.e. cancel the vote delegation to the party leadership. The votes can then be exercised at each vote itself or transferred to party members outside the party leadership circle.

... is focused on safeguarding the democratic processes within the party.

... approaches a topic without ideological blinders. Is focused on finding common ground and developing concrete, effective, and sustainable solutions.

... is focused in the internal discussion on the increase in knowledge of the participants.

... uses thematic summaries to inform everyone neutrally about the most important facets of a subject area.

... is transparent and committed to extending this transparency to the entire political arena and all public institutions.

## Does the party have to name itself "Proxy Party?"

Of course not. The term is precise as a specification but sounds more technocratic than likeable. The party can also have a completely different name, such as DDP "Direct Democratic Party" or DDTP "Direct Democratic Transparent Party."

## Are there representatives to vote against their convictions? So, is there some kind of party whip?

- The current practice in all parliaments is that a large proportion of representatives cannot vote according to their own convictions, even though they are officially only obliged to their voters. That is the logical consequence of the party whip. Only a few votes can be taken freely and only a few politicians dare to deviate from the line of their party.
- The proposed proxy system can ensure that the personal convictions of the deputies are again more in line with their voting behavior. By retaining and representing dissenting votes to the majority, the required level coercion is far lower than in today's system.
- The degree of legitimacy of this type of binding vote is higher because the instructions come from the party base.

## What to do if elected representatives vote differently than agreed?

If the voting weights of party members and elected representatives differ, individual representatives will be forced to vote against their convictions.

Therefore, only party members who strictly believe in and adhere to their role as proxy representative of party members should be selected. They know that they speak for the community/party members and not for themselves personally.

A representative who does not follow his instructions will be warned. He may get expelled from the faction or party if repeated several times.

**Is this party suitable as a coalition partner?**

The first step would be to join a coalition as a junior partner. Here, the Proxy Party would be a rather cumbersome partner. If you have to negotiate directly with the party base, you have to convince and cannot decide on your own. It is important to be convincing. That is laborious…but real democracy.

A potential positive side effect: grassroots democracy could have an infectious effect on the coalition partner.

But who says that the current way of forming a coalition is the best form of cooperation?

Wouldn't it even be better to come together to discuss a topic, to advance political and social projects in a solution-oriented way, instead of blocking each other's proposals, even if the proposed solutions are very reasonable? Austria is making very good progress with its transitional government in Summer 2019; politics without the party-political feud. Perhaps other countries parliaments should try that too.

**What happens if not enough party members come together to represent the population?**

A grassroots democratic party that does not represent a sufficient number of members has no sufficient justification. It must at least reach the threshold in order to decide on the extended party program.

## Does the idea of the Proxy Party work for countries with a two-party-system like the US and UK?

According to a 2018 poll 57% of Americans judged the Republican and Democratic parties to do such a poor job that a third major party is needed.[162]

But at first glance, it doesn't look pretty for a third party. Voting for third party candidates often means that you "waste your vote." Your candidate stands no chance against two candidates of larger parties. In the US presidential election, this means not giving the "party you dislike less" your vote, which might lead to your "worst choice" being elected. As already described, this leads to a "political vote" and heavily favors the two large parties and their candidates.

But what if the 42% of American voters registered as independent[163] would see a real chance for a new start? A fresh start with new party really representing them and not the 0.05% spending more than $10,000 in political campaigns.

But if you widen your view you can see the full picture that politicians don't like to mention:

---

162 https://news.gallup.com/poll/244094/majority-say-third-party-needed.aspx
163 Unbreaking America: A NEW Short Film about Solving the Corruption Crisis, https://youtu.be/TfQij4aQq1k

- The voter turnout in the UK general election was only 68.8%. The leading conservative party only received 5.7% more than the non-voters group.[164]

- The voter turnout in the 2017 US presidential election was only 58%.[165] The largest group was the group of non-voters!

But why does this group not vote? Three primary reasons:

1. They don't care enough about politics
2. They don't think that their vote can lead to any real change
3. They don't want to lend the corrupt system credibility by giving their vote

But what if those non-voters…

…would recognize that the new type of party is their only chance for a real democracy?

…would see a real chance not to "waste" their votes because ranked choice got introduced so that they can vote for their real preference and not strategically?

…would know that the election of the new party puts power in their hands?

…vote two thirds in favor of the new party?

…half vote for the new party, along with some other voters who are tired of the established parties?

---

[164] https://en.wikipedia.org/wiki/2017_United_Kingdom_general_election
[165] https://guides.libraries.psu.edu/post-election-2016/voter-turnout

**What about the cooperation between Proxy Parties of different nations?**

A proxy party would be highly interested to cooperate with other proxy parties, nationally and also internationally. It would be highly interested in..

> .. getting high quality input on topics for the preparation of discussions and decisions (one by one building up a very good knowledge base)
>
> .. learning from other parties that already tried new processes, policies etc.

This model would offer a far more cooperative and efficient alternative to the current political system.

# 17. Main potential attack vectors and defensive measures

**Disruptions in the process of political opinion-forming**

The Proxy Party is focused on efficiently safeguarding democratic and information processes within the party.

Forming a political opinion is complex and difficult. If some members have not sufficiently familiarized themselves with a topic, the process is even more complex.

Members could make this process more difficult due to a lack of factual orientation. Potentially, "professional trolls" could become members and try to disrupt the process. And only a few troublemakers are sufficient to turn a discussion around. Their action decreases overall trust. Participants block, instead of opening…and no progress is achieved.

The Proxy Party is not a YES/NO decision party. Minority votes reflected in the vote count as well.

Countermeasures:

- The focus is on identifying common ground and determining which topics should be tackled together and how.

- The moderation of discussions must be subject to clear rules and should ideally be carried out by experienced facilitators.

- Numbers brought in as information must always be supported by credible sources.

- Discussions aim at increasing the knowledge of the members. The system and the rules must be designed in such a way that as many relevant but non-redundant contributions as possible are encouraged. To achieve this, the participants are subject to restrictions. Algorithms must be created that check whether attempts are made to manipulate the system, e.g. through collusion.

- In extreme cases, members who do not contribute to the objective formation of opinion but noticeably disrupt, can be switched to "mute" for the online discussion. A graded system specifies whether the party member receives a temporary ban for the entire subject area. Muting can only be initiated by the participants themselves. It is only carried out by the moderator if the behavior of the member clearly deviates from the rules. Rules for this have to be established. Differences in content cannot lead to exclusion.

- Speaking times at events must be strictly limited synonymously to the discussions in forums.

## Technical overload of the party members

Numerous topics and individual questions have to be dealt with. It will be a great challenge to select and prepare the right ones. It will be important to attract and keep many committed and professionally experienced members. Of course, external people can also be invited for the input phase. But it should be kept in mind that their contributions could follow their own agenda and provide selective information.

## Time constraints on elected representatives and experts

Many of today's political processes are (intentionally?) associated with a flood of papers to be worked through. Members often do not have enough time to deal with the matter. From a mixture of convenience and excessive demands, many elected representatives ultimately follow the voting recommendation of their party.

This excessive demand on the part of elected representatives is at least accepted in an approving manner. The member of parliament cannot fulfil his responsibility as a representative of his electorate.

The Proxy Party should ensure that all bills are thematically prepared as described in Chapter 13, point 3:

> 2-Page Introduction and facts
>
> 1-page sketch effect relationships
>
> 1-Page pro-argumentation
>
> 1-page counter-argumentation incl. risks
>
> 1-Page recommendation

Since most laws are passed at EU level, the EU should also be asked to prepare accordingly. This will enable elected representatives, despite the flood of laws, to get a good overview of the laws and to be well informed about every law, even if they are not experts.

Votes, which are not sufficiently prepared or for which too little time was available, should be rejected automatically by the Proxy Party. The party can refer to this irresponsible pressure and thematize this in the press.

## Bundled offers from other parties (aka "horse-trading")

Bundled voting is the "horse-trading" of democracy. They lead to a blurring of the clear outline of an individual vote.

Issues must be dealt with and voted on individually. In this respect, bundled votes must be rejected.

The question of bundling can be passed on to the party base. If the party agrees, the party can give consent to the controversial vote.

## Authentication and anonymous internal party votes

The Pirate Party has discussed the method of user identification for a long time. Should the users discuss and vote with clear names or with pseudonyms or even anonymously? On the one hand, there is an interest in knowing who is behind a proposal. On the other hand, the use of the system creates a database with political opinions of individuals. And as we know through Edward Snowden at the latest, these can be collected and can harm these individuals.

A few thoughts on this:

- The negative experience in social networks shows that anonymity tends to lead to a more confrontational discussion. The user feels secure behind the pseudonym or as an anonymous contributor and behaves more extreme.
- The delegation of votes to anonymous users is not unproblematic.
- On the positive side, anonymity ensures that more attention is paid to the argumentation than to the name or position of the person contributing.

A difficult subject on which there is no clear solution. A combined use of all three authentication options might be possible, depending on the person's sense of security. The only important thing is that the anonymous user cannot bypass the exclusion from a discussion by logging in again. If this is not possible, an anonymous login must be rejected, as this would allow an unhindered permanent disruption of all discussions.

One thing is clear: It must be ensured that only registered party members receive access to the system and not more than one each. This is the only way to secure the principle "one member = one vote."

# 18. Hasn't this been tried and failed with the Pirates Party?

I was often asked whether all this had not happened before. The argument is: The Pirate Party tried something similar and failed in Germany and other countries. So why should it work this time?

It is correct that there are certain parallels. It is no coincidence that I referred to the Pirate Party in the previous chapters. Especially the party's grassroots democratic claim and its liquid democracy system have the same basis. A closer look at the two approaches reveals important differences.

## 18.1 Reasons for the rise and fall of the Pirate Party in Germany

"Pirate Parties started cropping up in Europe in the mid-2000s. Although they were intrinsically antiestablishment — gleefully flying black pirate flags as their symbol — they initially were narrowly focused on a narrowly libertarian set of issues. Issues such as transparency, Internet freedom and copyright reform were at the core of their agenda. Still, in the political turmoil of the early post-crisis, these parties gained some momentum and Pirate candidates took office in a handful of European parliaments."[166]

---

[166] https://www.washingtonpost.com/news/monkey-cage/wp/2016/10/30/no-

Their most relevant win happened in Iceland where they made the 5% hurdle in 2013 in the national election and won 3 out of 65 seats in parliament. They received a just-in-time boost before the next national election shortly after the release of the Panama Papers. In 2017 they were polled as far as 40%, but "only" brought in 14.5% and 10 seats. Today they still have 6 seats.[167]

According to the website of the Pirate Party International, the Pirate Parties are active in more than forty countries.[168]

For the rest of the chapter, I take the German Pirate Party as example. Its rise and fall has been well analyzed.

## The rapid ascent of the Pirate Party in Germany

The German Pirate Party was founded on 10th September 2006. "Similar to other European countries, the German Pirate Party was very successful in the beginning. It succeeded in moving into a total of four state parliaments as well as the European Parliament. At the beginning of 2012, opinion polls showed that pirates nationwide were already at 14 percent."[169] In 2011, the party had almost 35,000 members.[170]

The party was perceived by many as a fresh opposition worth experimenting.

---

the-pirates-didnt-win-icelands-elections-heres-what-happened-instead/?utm_term=.e735cc714cea

[167] https://en.wikipedia.org/wiki/Althing

[168] https://pp-international.net/pirate-parties/

[169] Translated from: https://www.deutschlandfunk.de/zehn-jahre-piratenpartei-kentern-statt-entern.724.de.html?dram:article_id=365537

[170] Translated from: https://sz-magazin.sueddeutsche.de/abschiedskolumne/danke-fuer-die-stoerung-piraten-83625

"The Pirate Party was a coalition of social outsiders who believed in progress and facts and who posed simple questions with their new organizational tools: how do we want to make politics? And thus, questioned everything."[171]
"I perceived the basic mood among the people of Berlin during the election campaign in this way: 'Oh, please, we'll just vote for anything that offers a reasonable alternative."[172]

"The Pirates not only inspired young people for party politics, but also produced great political talents who are now continuing in other parties. To name only a few: Martin Delius and Julia Schramm with the Left, Christopher Lauer with the SPD, and Sebastian Nerz with the FDP. With their vehemence and the resonance they have generated on topics such as internet blocking, data privacy, or broadband supply, they have in the first place ensured that questions and voices of our digital everyday life are recognized in big parties, timidly but increasingly, and that citizen participation has become a popular catchword."[173]

The pirates did not make it into the Bundestag even in their best days. They have achieved a lot in the state parliaments.[174]

---

[171] Translated from: https://sz-magazin.sueddeutsche.de/abschiedskolumne/danke-fuer-die-stoerung-piraten-83625

[172] Translated from: Sascha Lobo, Christopher Lauer, Aufstieg und Niedergang der Piratenpartei, Position 1482

[173] Translated from: https://sz-magazin.sueddeutsche.de/abschiedskolumne/danke-fuer-die-stoerung-piraten-83625

[174] Translated from: https://www.piratenpartei.de/piraten-wirken/piraten-wirken-in-parlamenten/

## Current status in December 2019

At present, the pirates have neither a seat in the Bundestag nor in one of the state parliaments.[175] In none of the federal states are they believed to be able to rejoin them.

## Topics of the Pirate Party

- Shaping the digital revolution

- Enhancing data protection

- Opposing the surveillance and incapacitation of citizens by the state

- Adaptation of copyright law to the digital society

- Freedom of information and free exchange of knowledge, against internet blocking

- Citizen participation and transparency

- Unconditional basic income

- Local public transport without tickets.

## Structural difficulties created on the basis of the party statutes

- "Too short terms of office of the board members of only one year, resulting from the fear of abuse of power, made longer-term projects considerably more difficult and prevented continuity.

- Between party congresses, the lack of structures (such as district associations) meant that there were hardly any regulated opportunities for effective political influence for most members, which led to greater dissatisfaction and greater pressure to meet expectations.

---

[175] German source:
https://de.wikipedia.org/wiki/Sitzverteilung_in_den_deutschen_Landesparlament
en

- The fact that the payment of member dues was not regulated by direct debit authorization, as is customary with parties, led to a non-payer rate of around 40% in 2011 and up to 60% in 2013 - the money was painfully lacking for professionalization."[176]

- "The fatal fallacy of the pirates was that the extensive absence of formal hierarchies does not mean that there are no hierarchies. Instead, unofficial ones are created, which are much more difficult to deal with, especially in cases of abuse."[177]

- "The often violently demanded desire for flat hierarchies, the assertion that every district association and every local association was unnecessary bureaucracy, led directly to the exhaustion of the few functionaries and widened the gap between them and the active part of the party basis."[178]

- "In the case of the pirates, the statutes basically dictated that every pencil purchase had to be decided jointly. In other parties, this job is done by the Secretary General…The pirates had both Secretary General and Political Director, but no management. The office titles were merely designations, without any concrete distribution of tasks or power being associated with them. Therefore, a majority in the board was necessary for each project."[179]

**Failure to live up to the aspirations of grassroots democracy**

"The occasional party conferences as the only "supreme body," are anything but democratic. Only pirates whom are present decide there; always only a small part of the members. The big pirate promises of a "Liquid Democracy"

---

[176] Translated from: Sascha Lobo, Christopher Lauer, Position 512
[177] Translated from: Sascha Lobo, Christopher Lauer, Position 563
[178] Translated from: Sascha Lobo, Christopher Lauer, Position 810
[179] Translated from: Sascha Lobo, Christopher Lauer, Position 2330

(Permanent General Assembly), was not implemented - but exactly that was for many a great hope for a real change in the usual "doing party politics." But soon the plan came to a standstill in the dispute between the data protection activists and the transparency activists, who could not agree on whether one should have a say in voting with clear names or at least a comprehensible pseudonym, or completely anonymously."[180]

## Lack of professionalism

Christopher Lauer, member of the Pirate Party in the Berlin House of Representatives:

- "I also keep saying that after five years there are still members of the Pirate Group who have no idea what parliamentary procedure is like in a parliament."[181]

- "Many pirates were not prepared to do so, criticizes Lauer. These are computer nerds with a digital understanding of politics: for them, there is only right or wrong, zero or one."[182]

- "I quickly learned that political work must take place at a high level of quality …. Proposals must be very well supported; the government must be cornered with demands so that it must deal with the topic of what is being demanded. Our political work had to produce very concrete, feasible, and press-effective alternative concepts, otherwise it could simply be ignored."[183]

---

[180] Translated from: https://www.claudia-klinger.de/digidiary/2014/03/21/woran-sind-die-piraten-gescheitert/

[181] Translated from: https://www.deutschlandfunk.de/zehn-jahre-piratenpartei-kentern-statt-entern.724.de.html?dram:article_id=365537

[182] Translated from: https://www.deutschlandfunk.de/zehn-jahre-piratenpartei-kentern-statt-entern.724.de.html?dram:article_id=365537

[183] Translated from: Sascha Lobo, Christopher Lauer, Position 2122

## Team, teamwork, and talents

- "Political talents like Marina Weisband, Martin Delius or Christopher Lauer are few and far between in the Pirate Party."[184]

- "... a lot of members, who knew indignantly what would not work under any circumstances. But much less who wanted to work constructively and constantly on solutions."[185]

- "The Pirate Party initially lacked social balance in the discourse due to this form of tech-heavy monoculture. Non-technicians were severely under-represented (as were women and migrants). The party lacked a variety of perspectives."[186]

- "Only a money and time elite could afford to become anything. And even these could only remain so if they brought enough human robustness with them to endure the constant bombardment by members and the rest of the public."[187]

- "The telephone conferences, but also the face-to-face meetings, were always public, so that it was basically impossible for us as a body to communicate with each other in any kind of trusting way. At most, this took place in private, leading to extreme fragmentation of the board and its communication."[188]

- "In other parties, the hierarchical structure creates working groups that usually deal with one topic for the whole party. Within these groups, the different political opinions are represented, which then have to work out a suitable consensus. With pirates on the other hand, in controversial areas a group was often formed for each

---

[184] Translated from: https://www.deutschlandfunk.de/zehn-jahre-piratenpartei-kentern-statt-entern.724.de.html?dram:article_id=365537
[185] Translated from: Sascha Lobo, Christopher Lauer, Position 528
[186] Translated from: Sascha Lobo, Christopher Lauer, Position 700
[187] Translated from: Sascha Lobo, Christopher Lauer, Position 821
[188] Translated from: Sascha Lobo, Christopher Lauer, Position 977

attitude, so there was no pressure to reach a consensus. The fact that these groups communicated almost exclusively via the internet did not make it any easier to form opinions. The result was a manageable number of proposals for many political areas, which were hardly coordinated without anyone having an overview. Almost congruent motions were submitted, as were completely mutually exclusive ones."[189]

- "Around sixty people, who had previously worked exclusively for the party, now had to deal with additional parliamentary work. Thus, the active core of the Berlin Pirate Party had been absorbed by parliaments…At the same time, new members flooded the party, who were simply accepted without preliminary talks and orientation assistance and left more or less to their own devices."[190]

## Quarreling, especially on the personal level

- "…ten years of quarrel and strife. Below the belt. Behind locked doors as well as on publicly accessible web platforms. There were insults, critiques… and the amused public reads all of it, for instance on *Twitter* or *Facebook*…Just a few weeks after the pirates moved into the Berlin House of Representatives in 2011, they had to call in a mediator on behalf of their parliamentary group."[191]

- According to Martin Delius, a member of the Pirate Party in the Berlin House of Representatives, the internal disputes "never took

---

[189] Translated from: Sascha Lobo, Christopher Lauer, Position 1178
[190] Translated from: Sascha Lobo, Christopher Lauer, Position 2137
[191] Translated from: https://www.deutschlandfunk.de/zehn-jahre-piratenpartei-kentern-statt-entern.724.de.html?dram:article_id=365537

place on the basis of different content-related opinions, but always on a personal level."[192]

- "... a public de-solidarization is taking place - there is neither a culture of mistakes nor a culture of gratitude - there is a perpetrator protection reflex which expresses itself in statements such as 'You just need thicker skin'."[193]

- Martin Delius' impression is also that "the Pirate Party has never managed to form a basis for political discourse. Decisions, even by federal party congresses, have not been complied with by federal executive committees, working groups, or individuals; there was no political basis for conformity in the first place, the debate was not based on content, but on people; on the basis of this, no program development can be carried out; on the basis of this, no political majorities can be won, neither within the organization nor outside of it. And this, has to collapse."[194]

- "...the lack of functioning discussion spaces favored a shift of discourses and conflicts towards *Twitter*. And this in turn had a very unfavorable effect on the public perception of pirates."[195]..."Twitter is an incubator of social dysfunction [...] There is no room for nuances or deeper discussions. Anyone who makes the mistake of trying will find even a long, differentiated article distilled down to a half-true 140-character summary. And that, in turn, will be used as new food for the outrage porn on *Twitter*."[196]

---

[192] Translated from: https://sz-magazin.sueddeutsche.de/abschiedskolumne/danke-fuer-die-stoerung-piraten-83625
[193] Translated from: Sascha Lobo, Christopher Lauer, Position 2397
[194] Translated from: https://www.deutschlandfunk.de/zehn-jahre-piratenpartei-kentern-statt-entern.724.de.html?dram:article_id=365537
[195] Translated from: Sascha Lobo, Christopher Lauer, Position 2439
[196] Translated from: Sascha Lobo, Christopher Lauer, Position 2431

## Difficulties of communication and PR

- The pirates have made enemies among artists and other groups through their position on copyright. "The phrase "abolish copyright" did fit into the digital way of thinking of the pirates and was heard exactly like that at the base. In essence however, it was a misunderstanding that was very unfavorable for us and deliberately promoted by many. After all, we had an elaborate program at that time. This did not involve the abolition of copyright at all, but liberalization and adaptation to the digital age. This position was adopted at the party conference in Offenbach in December 2011. Among other things, we called for protection periods after the death of authors to be shortened or for certain state information to be freely available."[197] "We would have done ourselves a great favor if we had made it clear from the outset that we wanted to change copyright law, especially at the European level. But it seemed clear to very few party members that it could only be done at that level."[198] "At the time, my approach to the media was still rather naive, and I underestimated the strong impact of individual formulations."[199]

- Every second sentence by Nerz was therefore: "I can't say anything about that," or "The party hasn't positioned itself on this yet," or "We haven't developed a political stance yet." However, being perceived as refreshingly different, not having an immediate answer to everything as a party politician, was a novelty after the election, but it quickly became worn out. The journalists felt cheated …"[200]

---

197 Translated from: Sascha Lobo, Christopher Lauer, Position 1872
198 Translated from: Sascha Lobo, Christopher Lauer, Position 1889
199 Translated from: Sascha Lobo, Christopher Lauer, Position 1902
200 Translated from: Sascha Lobo, Christopher Lauer, Position 1683

- Scandals around the topic "denial of the Holocaust" or more precisely a very provocative entry of Bodo Thiessen as a freedom of speech fetishist and the investigation against Jörg Tauss on suspicion of child pornographic activities.[201]

- Tweets of members were "shitstormed as the statement of a pirate and scandalized by the press in other publics."[202]

- Martin Delius: "He was fed up to have to justify himself constantly for the conduct of individual pirates."[203]

## An internal and an external summary

The internal view: "The reason for the failure of the pirates however, which hovered above everything else, was - the absence of a vision and the absence of the personnel who could have transported this vision. Instead, there was only a technical vision, participation via the internet, and a negative attitude towards pirate functionaries. All other problems, from lack of structures to latent right-wing and sexist beliefs to verbal mincemeat accidents in the social media, arose from this meta problem."[204]

"Damn, pay attention to the structures. Be skeptical of those who demand participation or grassroots democracy without presenting an appropriate, thought-out concept. Ideals are useless if they are not cast in concrete forms. Take the Pirate Party as an example of how politics doesn't work."[205]

---

[201] Translated from: https://www.faz.net/aktuell/politik/wahljahr-2009/bundestagswahl/piratenpartei-erfolgreich-gescheitert-1853555-p2.html
[202] Translated from: https://www.claudia-klinger.de/digidiary/2014/03/21/woran-sind-die-piraten-gescheitert/
[203] Translated from: https://www.deutschlandfunkkultur.de/piratenpartei-wird-aus-dem-entern-ein-kentern.1001.de.html?dram:article_id=365645
[204] Translated from: Sascha Lobo, Christopher Lauer, Position 2978
[205] Translated from: Sascha Lobo, Christopher Lauer, Position 2991

The external view: "The story of the pirates is told to the end: A one-theme party hits the nerve of the time and a generation, gets unexpected attention because of its colorfulness and is then also interesting for classic protest voters with the promise: 'We are the others,' and is hoisted over the five-percent hurdles. But the real political processes paralyze the party and the mass influx of members tears it apart at the same time. The structures cannot keep up with the growth, the promise of the participation of all cannot be kept, a clear vision is not to be found. Thousands of new members bring thousands of new topics. The Pirate Party is downright trotted out by pure antis, by professional protesters, and pathological majority haters, finally also by disgusting anti-Semites and of course by bad sexists, simply by confused people of all kinds."[206]

**Summary**

Unfortunately, despite many good ideas and a lot of commitment, the Pirate Party did not manage to get into the German Bundestag or to establish itself permanently in the German state parliaments. The most important factors of success and failure were:

+ Fresh opposition

+ Perceived as different

+ Worth an experiment

+ Belief in progress and facts

+ Shaping the digital revolution

+ Technical vision, participate via the internet

+ Citizen participation as a central theme

---

[206] Translated from: https://sz-magazin.sueddeutsche.de/abschiedskolumne/danke-fuer-die-stoerung-piraten-83625

+ Against surveillance state

+ For transparency

+ Activation of young people for politics

+ Attractive for protest voters and voters who want something different


- Perceived as 1-topic party

- No perceived clear cohesive line

- No vision developed

- Promises of basic participation not kept (permanent general meeting not implemented)

- Many critics, but not constantly involved constructive member to get things done

- Many trolls (antis, professional protesters, misanthropists)

- Rejection of party officials

- Permanent criticism up to public personal attacks

- Much navel-gazing instead of solution-oriented work

- Using Twitter as a discussion platform

- Digital political understanding instead of realism

- Structure not scalable

- Periods of office of directors too short (one year only)

- Absent official hierarchies led to unofficial hierarchies

- Statutes which permit only joint decisions

- Missing structures such as district associations

- Underestimation of the effect of simple formulations on the press

- Non-statements for a too long time "I can't say anything about that."

- Missing drawing of boundaries for expression of party members (Holocaust denial as a statement of freedom of opinion)

- Missing political intuition and lack of crisis PR

- Too few political talents who can transport themes

- Lack of diversity of perspectives (most male techies)

- Lack of a trustworthy basis for communication between officials, as all meetings were open to the public

- Lack of coordination of topics and rules for reaching consensus

- Underestimation of the resources necessary for parliamentary work

- Understaffing in roles to welcome new members and their involvement

- High non-payer ratio for membership fees as result of the waiver of direct debit authorization

## 18.2 Self-reflection and outlook

Christopher Lauer, member of the Pirate Party in the Berlin House of Representatives: "Today I think it needs a combination: The legislative, political part of a political group should enable all members to have a broad say and participation. The executive part, when it comes to keeping the shop running or managing day-to-day business, should be organized hierarchically so that one can work effectively and without major friction losses."[207]

Martin Delius, member of the Pirate Party in the Berlin House of Representatives: "Yes, the Pirate Party experiment has failed. That doesn't mean that there isn't room for a new progressive project with a future-oriented background, where technology is no longer in the foreground, but rather to discuss and politically implement the society of the future. And I don't believe that the Pirate Party is recovering from the development that

---

[207] Translated from: Sascha Lobo, Christopher Lauer, Position 1618

has taken place in recent years."[208]

Karl-Rudolf Korte, party researcher at the University of Duisburg-Essen: "We have choosy voters, and when there are gaps in supply or power-arrogant exclusion of topics, there is always the opportunity to parliamentarize on these new issues via niches. There is nothing static, nothing rigid. There is a lot of movement, a lot of dynamism and that is also the chance for new parties to succeed in the future." [209]

## 18.3 Derived Success Factors for the Proxy Party's Action

As a fresh alternative with a grassroots democratic approach, the pirates had a good start. But the structural weaknesses in the organization led to the Pirate Party not being elected to the Bundestag and later shrinking into insignificance.

It is extremely regrettable that the Pirate Party, despite the admirable commitment of many people, has not managed to channel the creative will of its members - to a large extent - into constructive discussions. This clearly shows that it is precisely a grassroots democracy that needs structures and rules in order not to be primarily occupied with itself and to be able to act externally as a constructive force.

In community management the 90-9-1 distribution is a well-known rule. For the Pirate Party with a peak membership of 35,000 members this translates to:

350 members actively involved in the content creation

---

[208] Translated from: https://www.deutschlandfunk.de/zehn-jahre-piratenpartei-kentern-statt-entern.724.de.html?dram:article_id=365537
[209] Translated from: https://www.deutschlandfunk.de/zehn-jahre-piratenpartei-kentern-statt-entern.724.de.html?dram:article_id=365537

3,000 members who take part in votes and comment on them

A lot could have been achieved. I would even say that the potential was even higher. The spirit of optimism was in the air and the majority of the members had experience in the conception of systems due to their professional background.

According to my analysis, the main thing for the Proxy Party is to position and structure itself well and to manage the expectations towards members:

(a) Positioning of the party

A fresh, progressive alternative that is different because it is provably more trustworthy and transparent; questions many things, is based on facts, believes in progress, and wants to achieve positive change. Vision for solving problems that encompasses the most important consistent cornerstones for solving the largest problem areas: Environment/ Financial System/ Financing/Aging Society/ Technology/ Social/ Peace.

(b) Managing member expectations

Grassroot democratic co-determination of topics, content collation, and discussion on an objective basis. Division of roles. The implementation is carried out by the party leadership or the elected representatives. Clear message that constructive participants with their expert knowledge are required. Open minds, who want to participate in the discussion based on facts and without ideology, who want to support the party leadership and elected representatives in order to achieve positive change. Objective criticism is desired, especially constructive criticism. Personal attacks are not OK and will have consequences, such as a warning or temporary exclusion from the respective discussion. Emphasis on the difference to normal parties: no majority is needed, since the 1:1 weighting of votes will transfer to votes in parliament. Majorities are only necessary if topics are to be included in the core party program or the extended program or for the election of candidates.

(c) communication concept

Development of a communication concept before the party presents itself to the outside world. This will include simple formulations for the press.

(d) A statute that places value on grassroots democracy and efficiency

Statute which provides for a clear, democratic but efficient separation of duties. A standing general assembly. Normal terms of office of the boards of directors and regional structures.

In addition, internal rules must be drawn up on the following topics:

- Elaboration of the precise processes of finding topics and coordination for inclusion in the core program of the party and the extended party program. Establish rules for discussion and re-opening of topics.

- Development of general rules for the coordination of topics and consensus building.

- Clear drawing of boundaries for statements made by party members in public that are dangerous to the party (e.g. Holocaust denial as freedom of opinion statement).

- Development of a PR concept for crisis situations.

- Concept for welcoming new members, informing them according to individual needs, involving them and motivating them to participate actively.

- Determining that membership fees are collected by direct debit authorization.

## 18.4 How is the Proxy Party different from the Pirate Party?

The Proxy Party is similar to the Pirate Party because it also has a grassroots democratic approach and attaches great importance to transparency. The main difference between the two parties can be illustrated by three points:

1. The Proxy Party goes further than the Pirate Party in its grassroots democratic approach. It includes the representative's premium right, the right to vote. The voting results of the party base are reproduced 1:1 if possible, so that an optimal representation is achieved.

2. The Proxy Party does not start as a one-theme party. It will position itself at the start or at the latest in the first year on several socially relevant topics and come up with concrete proposals. In the best case, it will already outline an alternative positive social model in the first year, combined with concrete suggestions as to how this can be achieved.

3. The Proxy Party already thinks about the scaling of the implementation before its start, so that its claim and reality do not diverge too far. The Proxy Party is aware that there is a trade-off between grassroots democracy and transparency on the one hand and efficiency on the other. Responsibilities and processes must be clearly defined and implemented in an easy-to-use software assisted solution.

## Summary

The Pirate Party was a hope that unfortunately has not been fulfilled. Many committed members created a spirit of optimism and managed to come up with important political issues. They gave these topics attention in public debate. Unfortunately, the party did not make it into the German Bundestag. This was mainly due to a combination of the party's own claim to grassroots democracy and the inadequate underpinning of it with appropriate structures and processes. The centrifugal forces resulting from this tension have led the party to navel-gaze instead of progress.

It is important to learn from the mistakes of the Pirate Party. Well defined processes of proposal and discussion of topics as well as voting are very important. A sound basis will enable the party to foster the motivation of new members constructively and channel it effectively. It is important to combine optimal grassroots democratic co-determination with a high degree of transparency and an effective social impact.

## 19. Why isn't it enough to vote  for individual proxy members?

The alternative to the Proxy Party would be individual candidates who see themselves as directly elected proxy representatives. They are normally elected as direct candidates and, as described in Chapter 12, vote exactly as their voters determine.

In the US, there are already candidates who have promised to behave in elections as determined by their voters through a platform such as united.vote[210] or other digital platforms.[211]  One of them is David Ernst.[212] The book *Architecture of a Technodemocracy* outlines a framework for a democracy based on individual candidates.

At first glance, these directly elected individual proxy candidates are a good idea. They correspond to the ideal of direct democracy. But this direct

---

[210] https://liquid.us
[211] https://medium.com/@dallasjcole/kavanaugh-circus-is-latest-example-of-how-winner-take-all-decisions-warp-our-democracy-cb882a363c20
[212] https://techcrunch.com/2018/02/24/liquid-democracy-uses-blockchain

election has some disadvantages that majorly result from the current state of the political system:

1.  The single candidate system will take into account only the majority of a single constituency. This may result in the will of the voters not being expressed. Example: three constituencies with 100% and 49% and 48% approval. Result: One vote for and two votes against, although almost two out of three voters agree with the proposal.

2.  Individual candidates will be less successful in activating many voters and integrating them into everyday political life.

3.  The individual candidate will not be able to create many good quality templates to discuss them with his voters. He simply lacks the time. If this work can be distributed among several people, more can be done.

4.  One candidate alone has a far lower chance of attracting experts to provide better input and lead discussions.

5.  The candidate will be dependent on external systems. As an individual, he is not in a position to advance the development of platforms that he needs for efficient exchange with his voters.

6.  Individual candidates can be more easily ignored than a party that has passed the 5% hurdle.

7.  Individual candidates are perceived less intensively by voters and the media. They can spread the idea of direct democracy and transparency less successfully than an entire party that focuses on these issues.

## Summary

Proxy representatives who are elected with the direct first vote is a good innovative idea. But they will have far less resources available than a Proxy Party. They will be less successful than a well-organized party focusing on the same issues.

# Conclusion: It's about time

The current form of purely representative democracy does not satisfy its own standards. It does not represent large sections of the electorate but prefers those with high incomes. The established parties have become too dominant and have largely undermined democratic competition. The main focuses are shop window politics and being re-elected. I can't see a bold vision of the future (one exception for America: Andrew Yang). We have loads of challenges ahead. We have millions of politically interested people. But the interest in participating in an active involvement in politics is declining.

As I have pointed out, the weaknesses of the system are manifold:

1. The choice of even an approximate political direction, every four years, is insufficient.

2. It is democratically inadequate neither to ask the electorate directly on important issues nor to give them an effective opportunity to appeal.

3. Laws are often too weakly formulated in some places to enable a strong democracy. Many political systems lack a clean democratic basis: a clean separation of powers. This led to the established parties expanding their powers for their own benefit over decades.

4. The structures within the typical party contribute to a weakening of democratic representation.

5. The current purely representative political structures allow lobbyists and other stakeholders to exert too much influence on politics.

6. Anti-corruption laws often have decisive loopholes. They are inadequate. Effective regulations and controls on the allocation of posts after the term of office are largely lacking.

7. The surveillance state is being expanded further and further.

8. The media too seldom takes their role as a controlling and disclosing fourth power in the state.

Because of its weaknesses, we urgently need to improve our democratic system. New technologies can help to re-politicize citizens. They can enable them to participate in the development of solutions. This is urgently needed to meet our massive challenges. It is also needed to build societal consensus on the use of modern surveillance technologies that have the potential to undermine our democratic rights.

But this important work will hardly be tackled by the beneficiaries of the weaknesses of the current system. So, I suggest founding the Proxy Party as a new political competitor. The Proxy Party will take on issues of democracy and transparency. It will remain focused on these issues in the long term; held accountable by its members. It will be our parliamentary champion for true democracy.

In contrast to the current system, the Proxy Party's direct-democratic approach allows members a real say. It binds its elected representatives to the party basis. The party basis has a far lower risk, that their leadership alienates itself from it. Based on the objective internal discussions and their structured processing the work of the new party is very fact-oriented. It rejects paternalism and "supervised thinking." It enables party members to form their own opinion on a topic. The discussions come with a clear emphasis on effective solutions and less on political correctness.

The Proxy Party is focused on advancing issues objectively. Party tactics do not play a role. This factual orientation should attract qualified experts. They will join the discussions and strengthen the party's ability to find solutions. This leads to objectively better and holistic solution concepts.

The best thing is that the party's approach can be implemented in the current political system.

The Proxy Party approach makes it much more likely that a new party

> (a) can overcome the parliamentary hurdle (e.g. 5% in Germany) as it credibly and demonstrably represents the interests of its members.
>
> (b) will also act in the interests of citizens in the long term, as it empowers its members to hold it accountable and gives them the right to make decisions themselves.

The most promising alternative would be to merge several small parties into one direct-democratic party. With this approach, they would have a good chance of overcoming the parliamentary hurdle. Instead of dividing into several parties on the basis of different views, the actors could reflect on their common interests and advance these and democracy itself.

It might not look reasonable that countries with a two-party-system like the US and UK have a chance to change their systems. But if we count correctly, most of the voters didn't vote for a party, but didn't vote at all.

> What if they knew that voting for the new kind of party puts the power in their hands?
>
> What if two thirds of the non-voters voted for their only chance of real democracy?

What if half of the non-voters and few of the other vote for real democracy? Those voters that decided to go to the poll station and choose pork or beef even if they are vegetarians.

A success of the Proxy Party would put the other parties under positive pressure. The success of the Proxy Party might lead to a re-politicization of society and a direct-democratic transformation of the political system.

> "A great democracy has got to be progressive or it will soon too cease to be great or a democracy."
> -Theodore Roosevelt

His words gave us a warning and pointed us the way. Let us follow his advice!

**** I would be very pleased if you would give me honest feedback on my book,** my thoughts, and the idea of the Proxy Party. What was the favorite thing you took away from the book?

Your review will also help other readers find my book and the ideas.

If you like, you can also visit me on my website upgradingdemocracy.com to learn more about the idea.

Thank you.

-Peter

P.S.: Don't miss to read appendix IV. I promise you will find a lot of interesting ideas.

# ABOUT THE AUTHOR

Peter Monien is a "political refugee" from Germany who lives in Switzerland. He has become increasingly disenchanted with what politicians are deciding in the name of the People and are doing with public funds, mostly unknown to the electorates they pretend to represent. After the 2007 financial crisis (and the subsequent lack of accountability at every economic and political level) he has lost faith in mainstream politics.

Peter's attempts to understand what led to these catastrophic outcomes, which are evidently not in the best interests of the average citizen, drove him to become a systems thinker in order to better understand the complex interrelated and interdependent parts of our political systems, with a view to effecting urgent change.

In August 2018, Peter decided to step forward and develop a new, truly democratic counterproposal to the current entrenched political system.

This journey led him over the political precipice and into the abyss of current political systems, arriving at an analysis of their weaknesses in order to propose a range of possible solutions that play to the strengths of true democracy.

The results of his research and proposal for a new kind of grassroots democratic political party, the "Proxy Party", can be found in his book, "Upgrading Democracy".

Peter's broad background in banking, economics, business administration, including market development and sales, gives him a unique insight into business and communications systems. As systems thinker and co-founder and former board member of the largest German freelancer cooperative, Peter is uniquely equipped to formulate and deploy actionable ideas that positively impact large-scale organizations, institutions and processes. Since 2014, he has been looking into how decentralized systems can be applied to achieve these goals for a fairer and more egalitarian society. Many of his solutions can be found in "Upgrading Democracy".

Additional information about his idea can be found on his website upgradingdemocracy.com.

# Annex I - Support for direct-election candidates

- When preparing candidates, it will be important to select the right candidates and provide them with massive support.

- Formulations that succinctly describe the idea of the proxy party must be intensively tested internally and externally in advance.

- Enabling the experience of the party
    - Prepared basic topics including elaborations (provide discussion paper), so that citizens can experience what the new type of policy could look like
    - Mock-up (executable sketch of a program) or prototype of a new internal voting system that can be presented on a tablet or smartphone

- Pre-tested election materials (internal and external) that convey the new party's message briefly and memorably. Possibly funny or more serious.

- Short, easily quoted, crisp sentences ("sound bites") that accurately outline the fundamental positions of the party.

- Accompanying materials, which offer interested citizens an introduction to the new alternative of grassroots democratic politics.

- Accompanying personalized videos (general intro, at the end a message of the direct candidate

# Annex II - Initial ideas on the process
# for thematic proposals

Overview of the submission of a topic proposal and the preparation path; whereby the personal contribution of committed members and good preparation ensure that topics are dealt with more quickly:

Stage 1: Suggested topics

Enter a topic with an introduction and the reason why this topic is important and should be dealt with by the Proxy Party. Minimum 1 page, maximum 2 pages.

→ Vote on inclusion of the topic by 50 randomly selected members. The quality of the proposal decided is critical to transfer it to the next stage.

Level 2: Draft topic

A first draft can be provided by the originator for approval. The proposer of the topic can organize further participants from the community who are interested in this special topic.

→ Vote on the inclusion of the topic by 250 randomly selected members. The quality of the input is an important factor to make it to the next stage.

Level 3: Official development of topics

Official elaboration by a virtual working group with topic experts, which has the goal of creating a verified voting template. Official appeal to all members who consider themselves to be topic experts or well informed to participate in the draft. 6 pages.

→ The result is an audited voting template.

Stage 4: Audited basis for reconciliation

→ Basic information for all members, basis for discussion among members (see point 3)

Stage 5: Possible adaptation of the voting template due to the broader discussion

→ Basis of voting

# Appendix III - Mini Publics, Example: AmericaSpeaks

"The work of AmericaSpeaks began with a clear and compelling vision: to reinvigorate American Democracy by engaging citizens in public decision-making that impacts their lives the most. For nearly two decades, the organization brought this vision to life. Through 150 projects that engaged more than 180,000 people and touched thousands more, AmericaSpeaks repeatedly broke new ground and achieved real results across the U.S. and around the world."[213]

"On entering the venue, citizens are faced with a series of small tables, each with a networked computer, electronic keypads for all participants and large video screens. Typically, participants are broken into demographically diverse tables of ten to twelve citizens, each with an independent facilitator.

Each table uses the networked computer to offer ideas and comments as their discussions progress. These are quickly collated and synthesized by a specialist team who distil comments from tables into themes that are presented back to the room via the large video screens, either for further comment or votes. The electronic keypads provide for instant voting. The large video screens present data, themes and information in real time for instant feedback.

---

[213] http://www.americaspeaks.org/

America Speaks runs these events only where there is commitment from decision-makers to attend and respond to the outcomes."[214]

---

[214] Graham Smith, Democratic Innovations: Designing Institutions for Citizen Participation (Theories of Institutional Design), p. 145

# Appendix IV – Other politically important topics

You can find many topics listed in Chapter 13. These are additional.

For the topics listed, it is important to me that it is not about whether I stand behind the individual topics. It is rather about their importance and the neglection by short-term oriented politicians.

The reader should judge for himself if one of the parties in the parliament of his country is likely to pick up these topics listed below. If you want to deal with our common problems and have a better meta structure, I recommend the Podcast "Creating a Humanist Blockchain Future" No. 51 on existential risks with Daniel Schmachtenberger.[215]

**Transparency & Democracy & Efficiency - Fundamentals**

Some basic considerations should be made. Some ideas on these topics would be:

- How much state is required? How much regulation? Can e.g. the bureaucracy be largely reduced (far more than 50%)?
- Efficiency Measurement Act, which stipulates that a meaningful measurement of efficiency must be made for all public services and that their results are to be published.

---

[215] https://thebitcoinpodcast.com/blockchain-future-2-19/

**Transparency & Democracy & Efficiency - Parliamentary operation and parliamentary services**

Many parliamentary processes are not structured particularly democratically. Some countries don't pay their representatives enough to be independent. Some pay far too much to the established parties and thus cement the status quo. Some ideas on these topics would be:

- Representatives should pay into the normal social funds, especially the pension funds. Many don't seem to care about these as they benefit from special pension funds that allow them to achieve a pension in a couple of years that a normal worker can't achieve in a lifetime.

- Laws concerning the financing of the parties or the members of parliament (resolution on their own behalf) will not come into force until the next legislative period.

- Reduction of the number of members of the German Bundestag to 400 members.

**Transparency & Democracy & Efficiency - European Union**

There is a significant lack of transparency in the political system of the EU. Some ideas on these topics would be:

- Brutally honest list of the benefits and opportunities of the EU and its disadvantages and risks.

- Meeting of EU countries and discussion on a new EU treaty. If the level of discussion reaches a 2/3 majority, then individual countries can join the new treaty if their populations agree to it in a direct vote. Even better would be to convene a European Citizens' Convention, half of whose representatives would be directly elected by the citizens, according to national and half transnational lists. A live broadcast of the debates in all EU languages and the publication of drafts, working papers and progress reports are available on the Internet. Several constitutional alternatives will be made available. These will be presented to citizens for selection with recommendations. Citizens can submit additional constitutional articles if one million citizens sign. The Constitution comes into force when a majority of the EU population and a majority of two-thirds of the states agree. Throughout the very transparent process, online surveys, telephone interviews, opinions from civil society organizations and citizens' councils (determined by lot) are often sought in order to strengthen participation and identification.[216]

## Transparency & Democracy & Efficiency - Elections

The persistence of party candidates and incumbents of positions is high. The system needs to be changed to bring much-needed personnel changes. Some ideas on these topics would be:

- Internal secret party internal primaries mixed with a personalized proportional representation system in which voters in the constituency and on the national list have the choice of several candidates from the same party. Each voter has two times five votes and can distribute these arbitrarily to candidates.[217] As a result, especially newcomers have a much better chance.

---

[216] Translated from: Ute Scheub, Die unvollendete Europa Demokratie, p. 78 and 80

[217] Translated from: Gregor Hackmack, Demokratie einfach machen: Ein Update für unsere Politik, p. 69

- Funding system for liquid democracy delegates, typically matter experts, with a publicly financed voucher of e.g. five Euro per month, which can be divided into 25 subject areas.[218]

## Transparency & Democracy & Efficiency - Offices

Party members are disproportionately represented in public office. The parties have decidedly too much influence on public organizations. Some ideas on these topics would be:

- No creation of additional positions for public officials one year after the election and one year before the next official election date.
- The share of party members in the population determines the maximum of public offices on all levels given to party members.

## Money, tax, financial and economic system

The growth-orientation of the economy, which is the easy answer for the elected officials, leads to malfunctions. The system purely fixated on increasing the gross national product creates existentially threatening side effects (externalities), that can turn the earth uninhabitable for humanity and many other species.

The current monetary system and its (mal)function has led to loss of value, huge speculative bubbles, expensive housing, and redistribution to the top, etc. For some years, experts expect the system to be so overstretched that an even more extreme crisis than in 2007/2008 is only a matter of time. It's time to put the system on a healthier basis. Some ideas would be:

---

[218] https://medium.com/@memetic007/making-liquid-democracy-work-pay-the-delegates-bd813a9cb60a

- Questioning the simple answer of growth orientation of the economy[219] and discussion of an economy that, without growth, causes greater prosperity effects for the vast majority of the population without making the planet uninhabitable and ourselves sick.

- Questioning the false dichotomy state/private enterprise. Addition of the "Commons" (common property) as third option. Conversion of a part of the economy into these Commons.[220] In 2009 Elinor Ostrom was awarded with the Nobel Prize. She demonstrated that resource arrangements commonly governed by their users are more efficient. Promotion of technological platforms for Commons. Support for start-up consulting and training of self-managing non-profit units managing common property.

- System change to a functional separation in banking not mixing in the high risks of Investment Banking business for the rest of us leaving the casino for those that want to visit it.

- Challenge our monoculture monetary system and its impact on our daily economic activities (pro-cyclical creation of money, short-term thinking, compulsive growth, increased income disparities, reduction in social capital) and the vulnerability of the system. Complementing the existing monetary system with a focus on urgent social issues:
  - How do we raise money for old people once we're older?
  - How do we provide billions of people with livelihoods if technological progress creates far fewer jobs than it makes obsolete?
  - How can we get companies to get into long-term thinking?
  - How can we prepare for a global financial crisis?

---

[219] https://positivemoney.org/publications/escaping-growth-dependency/
[220] https://primer.commonstransition.org/1-short-articles

Examples of solutions from a report by the Club of Rome, whose short description can also be found on the website[221] of Grandparents for the Future.

- Initiatives of NGOs: Doraland, Wellness Tokens, Natural Savings

- Initiatives of state institutions: Torekes, Biwa Kippu, Civics (regional), ECOs (national, European)

- Business Initiatives: C3[222] (regional, national), Trade Reference Currency Terra[223] (global), blockchain-based solutions for liquidity which will only create new money if there is a value behind it as collateral

- Bitcoin (recommended reading: *The Bitcoin Standard*)[224]

- Acceptance of anonymous Digital Cash as "Cash—and in an increasingly digital world, electronic cash—is a tool that law abiding private individuals can use to protect their privacy, autonomy, and ultimately their dignity. It should not just be tolerated, but fostered and celebrated. Not only do its benefits outweigh costs, it is a check that individuals may wield over abusive intermediaries. It will help ensure we do not lose our open society."[225] A good article[226] about this topic from Alex Gladstein can be found on Medium.

• Sovereign Money system (providing financial security to every citizen, reduction of speculative bubbles, extensive debt reduction

---

[221] https://grandparentsforthefuture.wordpress.com/2013/01/05/economics-creating-a-monetary-ecosystem/

[222] http://www.worldacademy.org/program-page/commercial-credit-circuit-c3

[223] https://wiki.p2pfoundation.net/Terra

[224] Saifedean Ammous, The Bitcoin Standard: The Decentralized Alternative to Central Banking

[225] https://coincenter.org/files/2019-02/the-case-for-electronic-cash-coin-center.pdf

[226] https://medium.com/@alexgladstein/the-moral-case-for-lightning-a-global-private-payment-network-9b232019a75b

of the state budget) instead of the present fractional reserve system. The Swiss were able to vote on this in June 2018.[227]

- Change to a system of "Free Money" creating money when the economy grows to keep prices stable. Distribution to all private persons as social dividend. This doesn't involve the creation of debt and doesn't drive asset bubbles. Option to be able to create anonym money.[228]

- Change to a system of mutual credit where all money comes into being through a transaction and perishes in its absence as it is currently used in LETSystems and e.g. described in the book *Sacred Economics*.[229]

- Shift to a gift economy and introduction of a demurrage currency that is losing 5 to 8% of its value each year as described in the book *Sacred Economics*. This is accompanied with levies on land, extraction of natural resources, the electromagnetic spectrum and other sources of economic rent. These levies would be paid out as a social dividend to all citizens. The approach promises an end to the inherent growth pressure of our current money system. It is a sustainable, long-term foundation for a permanently nongrowing economy that has the potential to end the drawdown of social and natural capital.

- Unconditional basic income (social participation in progress instead of degrading social security practice, inefficient incentive systems of extra income, etc.). Experiment with a town or region with 10,000 to 20,000 people over 5 years to receive relevant results on the behavior of residents. What people say they do, and what they actually do, often diverges widely. The scientist Ray Kurzweil, who

---

[227] https://www.vollgeld-initiative.ch/english/
[228] http://emancipationparty.org/reforms/free-money/
[229] https://wiki.p2pfoundation.net/Mutual_Credit

has been right with most of his future predictions, expects the introduction of the unconditional basic income in the richer countries of the world in the early 2030s and that all citizens will be able to live a good life.[230]

- Supplement the basic income with a Social Credit System, as proposed by the US presidential candidate Andrew Yang in his book *The War on Normal People*. This is based on a time when the banking system, according to him, "would tie together communities and give people a way to both generate value regardless of how the market regards their time."[231]

- Financial transaction tax (Tobin Tax)[232] on all international foreign exchange transactions. This would limit short-term speculation to currency fluctuations and be a source of income for development funds or an unconditional basic income.

- Ban on uncovered credit default swaps (CDSs), which, according to investor legend Warren Buffet, are "financial weapons of mass destruction", especially those on agricultural commodities.

- Reorganization of the VAT system to steer consumption and support the achievement of key challenges: Product/service has a positive impact on the achievement of the objectives or a neutral or negative one with rates of taxation of e.g. a reduced tax rate of 7%, a normal tax rate of 19%, and an increased tax rate of 22%. If a shift

---

[230] https://www.ted.com/talks/the_ted_interview_ray_kurzweil_on_what_the_future_holds_next

[231] Andrew Yang, The War on Normal People: The Truth About America's Disappearing Jobs and Why Universal Basic Income Is Our Future, p. 194

[232] https://youtu.be/H2A2x4SSq0E, John McMurtry - "It's proof positive of the cancer system."

to VAT as a primary way of public funding is made, the VAT rates for individual goods may be much higher.

- Conversion of the determination of the income tax rate according to the Swiss model. The federal states and municipalities can set their own tax rates with a defined minimum rate yet to be determined. They receive their money directly from the taxpayer.

- Change in the fiscal equalization facilities between federal states, so that each state only has to receive at least 90% of the average. This gives the federal states more incentive not to spend money where there is none.

- Funding (only for start-up and training) of self-governing non-profit entities that manage commons.

- Change of patent law and copyright law so that innovation is possible on a broader basis. Reduction of copyright and patent protection to five years plus renewal. The price for a one-year extension starts moderately with $100 and doubles every year. This would be $51,200 for the tenth year and $1.6m for the 15th year. The multiplication factor could be subject to a classification of rights whereby very beneficial inventions for humanity could have a higher multiplier, e.g. a quadrupling or sextupling per year. Revenues for the renewal of the rights will be transferred to a pool, which will pay out an "IP dividend" to all residents (partly financing an unconditional basic income).[233] This idea is particularly relevant in connection with new inventions that lead to the automation of work.

---

[233] https://medium.com/basic-income/the-zombification-of-intellectual-property-and-the-tool-that-could-finally-reform-it-2ec037309837

- Provide scientific research results for free if these were financed by public funds as well as software developed with public money.[234]

- Open Creation: $10 per month for each citizen to exclusively fund the creation of intellectual property for non-rivalrous goods. Combined with kickstarter like platforms with a robust reputation system and custodial services.[235]

## Support of developing nations

Despite billions of dollars and euros, most of the countries of the African continent have not become thriving landscapes. The previous approach has missed its official goal of developing these regions. Some ideas on these topics would be:

- Change at least ¾ of payments to proven impact-oriented support to developing countries, as well as debt cancellation (payment against achievement of objectives and a partial relocation of funds to those countries that have demonstrably achieved this). Introduction of effective external controls and control of controllers.

- Transforming trade relations and treaties and tariffs so that developing countries have a good opportunity to build their own industries. Karl-Martin Hentschel of "More Democracy", proposes a fair-trade model that provides for free trade without customs duties and only provides for surcharges if the international standards on human rights, environmental standards, etc. are not met. This would lead to increased efforts by all countries to improve their position in these areas.[236]

---

[234] Translated from: https://t3n.de/news/sascha-lobo-breites-buendnis-code-1148918/
[235] http://emancipationparty.org/reforms/open-creation/
[236] Translated from: Ute Scheub, p. 57

- Support the development of transfer systems that cost less than 1% of money transfers to low-and-middle income countries (currently about 6.9%). With a transfer volume of $549 bn in 2019, this will generate over $32 bn more purchasing power in these countries.[237]

- International ban on sanctions restricting the delivery of food and medicine.

## Environment

About everyone should know by now that the world's population consumes more resources each year than sustainable. Some people will know the newly named "Anthropocene", which describes the massive escalation of harmful effects caused by mankind. This will cause, among other things, the sixth major mass extinction. The last mass extinction was triggered 65 million years ago by a huge asteroid. The current mass extinction is due to rapidly spreading humanity and our economic system. Everyone should also be aware that we are progressively depriving our own livelihoods as we continue our current path. Hoping that the complex climate system will not have any self-reinforcing effects that accelerate our departure, is not a valid strategy. Neither is ignoring the cumulative accumulation of environmental toxins. Some ideas would be:

- Focus our attention: Conversion and consolidation of existing models under the doughnut model of Kate Raworth, which combines environmental and social aspects.[238] Extension to the

---

[237] https://www.worldbank.org/en/news/press-release/2018/12/08/accelerated-remittances-growth-to-low-and-middle-income-countries-in-2018

[238] https://www.ted.com/talks/kate_raworth_a_healthy_economy_should_be_designed_to_thrive_not_grow?language=en, TED Talk: A healthy economy should be designed to thrive, not grow, Kate Raworth

consideration of the enrichment and exhaustion cycles. We should strive for optimization without creating harmful externalities. As seen in a diagram of the donut development statuses of the countries, each country is a "developing country".[239]

- Gradual conversion of production to reusable or completely recyclable components (circular economy).

- Conversion to a stable decentralized renewable energy supply.

- No restriction of market access or trade in self-produced seeds or restriction of their use. No privatization or monopolization.[240]

**Value system and discussion culture**

Political correctness goes too far when it no longer addresses existing problems or foreseeable problems, thus blocking appropriate solutions. Practically every decision comes with negative effects. These must be discussed. Thinking blocks are also solution blocks. Wishful thinking only creates a better reality to a limited extent. A "We can do it," without the support of suitable measures will not be successful. Some ideas:

- Use the same measuring stick (morally and in international politics)

- Open-ended analysis and discussion of policy challenges. Moral arguments should be only discussed after the facts have been collected. In the case of doubt, the so-called "Political Correctness" should be postponed since solutions must take precedence over sensitivities. This is especially true when facts are disagreed upon, underlying mechanisms are negated, or solutions are blocked.

---

[239] https://www.kateraworth.com/2018/12/01/doing-the-doughnut-at-the-g20/
[240] Translated from: https://unserplanet.net/saatgut-monopol-und-elend-von-afrika-bis-europa/?fbclid=IwAR2eOswemfAXVwXb2byke30Af3WREcHV-EMhvOh8P9IEibM31GXV1l0Iwws

- Discussion of the actions of individuals and organizations that we, as a society, can accept or tolerate.

- How can we achieve less ideological and group-oriented thinking (Identity Politics) and more solution-oriented and socially oriented instead?

- Removal of all signs of faith in public buildings to make it clear that the highest authority is the constitution and that the civil servant is obliged to obey it.

- Critical examination of the special rights of churches in Germany in the course of their lesser importance over time.

## Impact of the technological revolution on society

Technical unemployment is real and already here. We face a pandemic of economic insecurity.[241] Artificial intelligence, blockchain, robotics, the Internet of Things, Nano technology, biotechnology, and many other exponential technologies are currently changing our lives. Studies say many of our current jobs will be lost over the next decade. According to McKinsey[242], 400 to 800 million jobs will be lost worldwide by 2030. A *New York Times* article[243] from January 2019 on automation, reveals why this will be the case. This change is accelerated by the historically low interest rates as they make the "technical replacement investment case" more attractive.

To be a good investment, new technology doesn't have to replace the full job an employee is currently carrying out, but only has to cover individual tasks

---

[241] https://medium.com/basic-income/the-real-story-of-automation-beginning-with-one-simple-chart-8b95f9bad71b

[242] https://www.mckinsey.com/featured-insights/future-of-work/jobs-lost-jobs-gained-what-the-future-of-work-will-mean-for-jobs-skills-and-wages

[243] https://www.nytimes.com/2019/01/25/technology/automation-davos-world-economic-forum.html

more efficiently. Progress in one domain can be mostly directly transferred to other domains. Successes in Work Area A can be transferred to work Areas B, C, D, and E. Information technology is a universal technology and will affect all areas. Machines and algorithms are much further advanced than the average citizen currently imagines. They are developing rapidly[244] and will also affect highly qualified white-collar jobs.[245]

Autonomous taxis and trucks[246] and warehouse robots[247] are already familiar to most. Other examples that may surprise some readers are: barista[248], recruiter[249], programmer[250], news anchor[251], journalist,[252] artist (painter),[253] scriptwriter[254], composer[255], lawyers[256] (especially file searches), food preparation and restaurant services,[257] and many more. Blockchain

---

[244] https://youtu.be/o0pqSKfn8FU and  https://hackernoon.com/ai-in-five-fifty-and-five-hundred-years-part-one-e630058b547f

[245] Automation entering white-collar work, https://youtu.be/YbrfQaHsC6U

[246] https://www.youtube.com/watch?v=sIlCR4eG8_o&feature=youtu.be

[247] https://www.youtube.com/watch?v=4DKrcpa8Z_E&feature=youtu.be

[248] https://www.washingtonpost.com/technology/2019/03/22/baristas-beware-robot-that-makes-gourmet-cups-coffee-has-arrived/?noredirect=on&utm_term=.8a50c2bb7e1f

[249] https://www.forbes.com/sites/forbescoachescouncil/2018/08/10/10-ways-artificial-intelligence-will-change-recruitment-practices/#32f7c3ab3a2c

[250] https://futurism.com/military-created-ai-learned-to-program

[251] https://www.cnbc.com/2018/11/09/the-worlds-first-ai-news-anchor-has-gone-live-in-china.html

[252] https://medium.com/the-new-york-times/the-rise-of-the-robot-reporter-dccf42813c49 und https://medium.com/futuresin/ai-tools-are-getting-too-dangerous-to-release-to-the-public-2565572e1f5d

[253] https://www.dailymail.co.uk/sciencetech/article-4652460/The-AI-artist-create-painting-style.html and https://medium.com/abovethefold/the-ai-art-gold-rush-is-here-a3dda143563

[254] https://arstechnica.com/gaming/2016/06/an-ai-wrote-this-movie-and-its-strangely-moving/

[255] https://futurism.com/the-worlds-first-album-composed-and-produced-by-an-ai-has-been-unveiled

[256] https://hackernoon.com/20-top-lawyers-were-beaten-by-legal-ai-here-are-their-surprising-responses-5dafdf25554d

[257] https://www.techemergence.com/ai-in-restaurants-food-services/

technology has a massive impact on all auditing professions[258], as the functionality, comparable to an automated notary service, will replace many services.

As presidential candidate Andrew Yang wrote:

> "The test is not 'Will there be new jobs we haven't predicted yet that appear?' Of course there will be. The real test is 'Will there be millions of new jobs for middle-aged people with low skills and levels of education near the places they currently reside?'"[259]

Many countries are discussing the abolition of cash. This step would make payments more efficient and save the financial system a lot of money. But purely digital money also allows negative interest rates to be enforced and the money to be blocked or in extreme cases to be confiscated. It would also provide an excellent basis to effectively monitor citizens. The precursor of such a system has been around for many years with WeChat, which has become popular in China for its ease of use and performance. The Chinese state is currently supplementing this with a "Social Credit System"[260] which gives citizens grades that also depend on their behavior and friendships and is also used to sanction citizens. Purely digitally available not-anonymous money, also has the advantage for the government that it can be used to control its citizens. Supplemented with high-resolution cameras and face recognition software, a surveillance state can be efficiently operated.

On the other hand, technical progress also offers fantastic opportunities. Authors such as Peter Diamandis and Steven Kotler write in their book

---

[258] https://www2.deloitte.com/us/en/pages/audit/articles/impact-of-blockchain-in-accounting.html

[259] Andrew Yang, The War on Normal People, p.74

[260] https://www.businessinsider.com/china-social-credit-system-punishments-and-rewards-explained-2018-4?r=US&IR=T

*Abundance,* that we can meet the basic needs of all of humanity by 2030. This is achieved through: Artificial Intelligence, Robotics, Digital Fabrication, Synthetic Biology, and other exponential technologies.[261] So-called "moonshot projects," have the potential to advance all of humanity and solve many, if not all, of our problems.[262]

> "We are racing toward a world of abundance, and we are going to be increasing the quality of life for everyone on this planet."
>
> -Peter Diamandis, cofounder and executive chairman of Singularity University

The only question is *how* we will distribute this increase in productivity. Will income and wealth distribution become even more spread? Or, will we succeed in making technical progress even more effective for the well-being of all?

Politics is asked to recognize the changes that are coming our way and to use them as a positive force for society. Some ideas would be:

- Progressive focus of politics on the basis of scientific knowledge, rational consideration and problem-solving, instead of symbolic policy, symptom control and inconsistent individual decisions.

- More intensive use of technological progress to improve the lives of all. Discuss a vision that aims to gradually make available (free of charge) all the goods and services fundamental to human prosperity. This will be achieved primarily through technological innovations and the resulting price reductions.

---

[261] YouTube: Ray Kurzweil, What Is the Future of Capitalism?, https://youtu.be/CX318Lr2eoo and Peter Diamandis, Imagining the Future: The Future of Humanity, https://youtu.be/7XrbzlR9QmI
[262] http://moonshotsupdate.com

- Jobs will disappear much faster than new jobs will be created. Are the current mechanisms sufficient if the unemployment rate reaches 20%? What can substitute for regular employment (see "unconditional basic income")?

- Do we want to force people to work or into a social welfare system when they are unable to adapt quickly enough to new challenges or that do not want to work? Should we force them to do so? But what happens if they don't not create enough value to earn the legal minimum hourly rate? Which activities, apart from a paid work activity, can create a fulfilling life (meaning / ability & recognition / variety / connection / development / part of something bigger)?[263]

- Conversion of education to truly relevant skills such as "learning to learn", making informed choices, and critical thinking. Developing other skills: agility and adaptability, initiative and entrepreneurship, effective communication, information analysis, curiosity and imagination, problem solving, creativity, and cross-network collaboration. Holistic teaching of topics, showing connections increases the interest of the students. Subjects such as history, moral philosophy, behavioral economics, probability theory, neurology, IT, and literature could be taught in a far more practical and impressive way.

- Media education: distinction between information, disinformation, and propaganda. What are the requirements for good research? How can I do this myself?

- General discussion on the consideration of "monitoring vs. informationnal self-determination" and strengthening of the legal rights to informational self-determination. One of the negative sides of man-

---

[263] https://www.entrepreneur.com/article/240441

controlled artificial intelligence is that it will always obey its owners. For example, a biometric bracelet (body functions and brain-waves[264]) can be very useful for monitoring health information and safety. The same functionality can also be used to establish or maintain the perfect dictatorship.

- Official acceptance of the use of anonymous digital payment options.

- Regulate ownership of data to prevent further concentration of power and wealth. Data is the wealth of the knowledge society.

## Other topics

More topics can be found in Chapter 13, which deals with the potential topics of a Proxy Party.

The technological developments soon allow us a life in abundance. The systems could be designed in harmony with the resources of the earth. But we are a long way from such a future and we're not even steering towards it. Politicians of the opposition have been using the phrase "The country is governed far below its potential." Often, however, they only mean that the wall should be painted blue instead of red. None of the established parties offers a bold vision and a viable way to realize it.

---

[264] https://www.ted.com/talks/nita_farahany_when_technology_can_read_minds_how_will_we_protect_our_privacy